MIRACLES—DO THEY STILL HAPPEN TODAY?

God Miraculously Saving People's Lives, Apparitions, Speaking In Tongues, Faith Healing

Edward D. Andrews

Christian Publishing House
Cambridge, Ohio

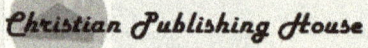
Professional Christian Publishing of the Good News

Copyright © 2015 Christian Publishing House

All rights reserved. Except for brief quotations in articles, other publications, book reviews, and blogs, no part of this book may be reproduced in any manner without prior written permission from the publishers. For information, write, support@christianpublishers.org

Unless otherwise stated, scripture quotations are from *The Holy Bible*, *Updated American Standard Version (UASV)*®, copyright © 2016 by Christian Publishing House, Professional Conservative Christian Publishing of the Good News!

MIRACLES—DO THEY STILL HAPPEN TODAY? God Miraculously Saving People's Lives, Apparitions, Speaking In Tongues, Faith Healing

Publishing by Christian Publishing House

ISBN-13: 978-0692423066

ISBN-10: 0692423060

Table of Contents

CHAPTER 1 Does God Step in and Solve Our Every Problem Because We are Faithful? 1

Praising God as the Grand Savior 1

Thirsting for God as a Deer Thirsts for Water 2

Why am I in Despair? 4

Wait for God 11

CHAPTER 2 Does God Provide Bible Absolutes or Guarantees In This Age of Imperfect Humanity? 14

They Sound Like Absolutes 15

CHAPTER 3 Are Miracles Still Happening Today? 20

Judging Your Own Case 25

A Brief Papal History 30

Alleged Evidence of Miracles 38

Purpose of Miracles 42

Miracles were Evidence of Change 44

The Purpose has Been Served 45

The Mark of True Christianity 46

CHAPTER 4 Is Faith Healing Scriptural 48

What is Faith Healing? 49

Does Faith Healing Work? 50

Is There Any Harm In Believing in Faith Healing? 51

Some Similarities Cannot Be Ignored ... 52

Jesus Heals 53

What Was the Purpose of Jesus' Healing? 55

God's Word is Alive 60

The New Earth: The Earthly Hope 62

CHAPTER 5 Is Speaking in Tongues Evidence of True Christianity? 69

What Was the Reason for the Speaking in Tongues? 69

Spread of Christianity in the first century 73

Modern-day Speaking in Tongues 73

What is the Real Force Behind Today's Speaking in Tongues? 78

Should Christians be identified by their ability to "speak in tongues"? 79

Is this really, what the Bible teaches? 86

As for Tongues, They Will Cease 86

Speaking in Tongues and Today's Christianity 89

Final Thoughts 90

CHAPTYER 6 Is Snake Handling Biblical? 92

Founders of Snake Handling 93

Snake Handlers Today and Practices 94

Risks of Snake Handling 96

Does not Mark 16:17, 18 (NKJ) show that 'snake handling' would be a sign that one is a believer? 97

Is This Really, What the Bible Teaches? 102

"Thou Shall Not Tempt the Lord" 103

What About Luke 10:19? 104

CHAPTER 7 How Are We to Understand the Indwelling of the Holy Spirit? 109

Jesus Promises the Holy Spirit 119

Paul told the Christians in Rome, ... 122

Paul told the Christians in Colossae, ... 124

vii

Paul told the Christians in Ephesus,..... 126

Bringing This Transformation About...133

CHAPTER 8 The Work of the Holy Spirit.. 136

The Work of the Holy Spirit 155

Bibliography 159

CHAPTER 1 Does God Step in and Solve Our Every Problem Because We are Faithful?

Praising God as the Grand Savior

Psalm 42 depicts for us the circumstances of a Levite, one of the offspring's of Korah, who found himself in exile. His inspired words can be very beneficial to us in preserving thankfulness for friendship with fellow Christians and continuing steadfastly while going through hostile conditions.

Thirsting for God as a Deer Thirsts for Water

The psalmist stated,

Psalm 42:1-2 English Standard Version (ESV)

¹ As a deer pants for flowing streams,
 so pants my soul for you, O God.
² My soul thirsts for God,
 for the living God.
When shall I come and appear before God?

A female deer cannot survive long without water. If water is low, the deer will risk its life going out of cover to get at the lifesaving water, even though she knows that the prey could attack at any moment. Like the deer that longs for water because it is a matter of life or death, the psalmist longed for God. The word "pants" in the Hebrew means "to have a keen, consuming desire for." His driving passion was not for people, possessions, or prosperity but for God."[1]

The Bible lands are a dry country, where the vegetation wastes away rapidly throughout the dry season, and water is a very valuable commodity, as it is limited in the extreme. That is why the Psalmist says that he was a 'soul thirsting for God.' He had been going without his essential spiritual needs being satisfied, that is the freedom of going to the sanctuary; therefore, he asks when he might again "appear before God."

He had been confined because of persecution, which prevented him from having contact with his fellow believers, which resulted in intense sadness, unhappiness and hopelessness, as verse three indicates.

---

[1] Anders, Max; Lawson, Steven (2004-01-01). *Holman Old Testament Commentary - Psalms: 11* (p. 224). B&H Publishing.

Psalm 42:3 English Standard Version (ESV)

³ My tears have been my food
    day and night,
while they say to me all the day long,
    "Where is your God?"

Because of this hostile situation, the Psalmist was depressed to the point of being unable to eat. Therefore, his 'tears were his food.' Yes, "day and night" tears would roll down his cheeks into his mouth. His isolation and distress were not enough, as his enemies aggravated his wounds by provoking, ridiculing, in a hurtful or mocking way, as they would say all day long, "Where is your God?" He needed to find a way to reassure himself during this time of difficulty, to not be overrun by sorrow and heartache.

Why am I in Despair?

Psalm 42:4-6 English Standard Version (ESV)

⁴ These things I remember,
    as I pour out my soul:
how I would go with the throng
    and lead them in procession to the house of God
with glad shouts and songs of praise,
    a multitude keeping festival.

⁵ Why are you cast down, O my soul,
   and why are you in turmoil within me?
Hope in God; for I shall again praise him,
   my salvation ⁶ and my God.

My soul is cast down within me;
   therefore I remember you
from the land of Jordan and of Hermon,
   from Mount Mizar.

Here we find the Psalmist not living in the moment of suffering, but rather remembering a time before he was in exile. He 'pours out his soul,' reaching the depths of his inner self with such passion, as he reminisces within about the former days. The Levite recalls in his mind what life was like when he was in his land, as he lived and worshiped with his brother and sister Israelites, as they walked "to the house of God," to celebrate the festival. Initially, these memories did not bring joy, but the pain of knowing they were a thing of the past, deeply missed.

Then, he asked himself, "Why are you cast down, O my soul and why are you in turmoil within me"? At that moment, he realized that his hope of salvation was not in himself, but In God. Therefore, the sweet memories truly brought him relief! He knew that if he patiently waited, God would act in his behalf. He then knew that his unfavorable conditions were not going to define his faith that, in time God would aid him in his time of need. When that moment would happen, he would "praise him" for 'his salvation' and being 'his God.' He might have been far removed from the sanctuary, but the Psalmist kept his God at the forefront of his mind.

If we ever find ourselves in difficult times, unrelenting times, we need to follow the pattern set by the Psalmist. We need to remember that God is well aware of our circumstances, and he will not forsake us. We must realize that the issues that were raised by Satan in the Garden of Eden, the sovereignty of God, the rightfulness of his rulership, and the issues raised by Satan to God in the book of Job, the loyalty of God's creatures, are greater than we are.

Proverbs 3:25-26 Lexham English Bible (LEB)

[25] Do not be afraid of sudden panic,
  or the storm of wickedness that will come.
[26] [Jehovah] will be your confidence
  and guard your foot from capture.

Before delving into the rest of Psalm 42, let us take a moment to establish what these verses do not mean. Should we understand that these verses or any others in Scripture teach that because we are wisely walking with God that he will miraculously step in to protect each servant personally from difficult times, diseases, mental disorders, injury or death? No. These sorts of miracles are the extreme exception to the rule. Of the 4,000 plus years of Bible history, from Adam to Jesus, with tens of millions of people living and dying, we have but a few dozen miracles that we know of in Scripture. Even in Bible times, miracles were not typical, far from it. Hundreds of years may pass with no historical record of a miracle happening at all.

If we are wisely walking with God, we can be confident that bodily disease, mental disorders, injury or early death is far less likely than if we were not. Moreover, we can draw on the resurrection hope. Does God miraculously move events to save us out of difficult times or miraculously heal us? Yes, he certainly can, but it is an extreme exception to the rule. He miraculously heals those who are going to play a significant role in his settling of the issues that were raised in the Garden of Eden.

What God's Word teaches us is this, that if we walk by using discernment and exercising sound judgment from Scripture, unless unexpected events befall us, we can be sure that we will not stumble into the difficulties that the world of humankind alienated from God faces every day. Conversely, the wicked do not have this protection as they reject the Word of God as foolish. In other words, Christians live by the moral values of Scripture, which gives them an advantage over those who do not. Therefore, God answers our prayers by our faithfully acting in behalf of those prayers, by applying Scripture in a balanced manner. If we have not taken in a deep understanding of God's Word, how can we have the Spirit inspired wisdom, the very knowledge of God to guide and direct us in our ways? Just because we are not being rescued when we feel that we should, this does not mean that we have lost faith, or that God is displeased. Even though the Psalmist had no doubt that Jehovah God was coming to his aid, he still experienced grief.

Psalm 42:7 English Standard Version (ESV)

[7] Deep calls to deep
   at the roar of your waterfalls;
all your breakers and your waves
   have gone over me.

Yes, the Psalmist's surroundings of his exile were very beautiful; however, they brought him back to the reality of his difficulty! Verse 7 may very well be describing the snow on Mount Hermon when it melts. Marvelous waterfalls are fashioned, which pour into the Jordan, causing it to increase in size. It is as though one wave is speaking to another wave. This extraordinary spectacle of power brought to the Psalmist's mind that he had been consumed by distress as if being overcome by a flood. Nevertheless, his faith in God does not waiver.

Psalm 42:8 English Standard Version (ESV)

[8] By day [Jehovah][2] commands his steadfast love,
> and at night his song is with me,
> a prayer to the God of my life.

There is no doubt in the Psalmist's mind that Jehovah God will engulf him with his

---

[2] Translations take liberties with God's personal name, by removing it and replacing it with the title LORD in all caps. There is no rational reason, or Scriptural grounds for doing so. In fact, Scripture shows just the opposite.—See the American Standard Version Isaiah 42:8; Malachi 3:16; Micah 4:5; Proverbs 18:10; Joel 2:32; Ezekiel 36:23; Exodus 9:16; Malachi 1:11; Psalm 8:1;148:3.

steadfast love, freeing him of anxiety. This will empower him to praise God in song and to offer a prayer of thanks 'to the God of his life.'

The Korahite Levite thinks,

Psalm 42:9-10 English Standard Version (ESV)

⁹ I say to God, my rock:
   "Why have you forgotten me?
Why do I go mourning
   because of the oppression of the enemy?"
¹⁰ As with a deadly wound in my bones,
   my adversaries taunt me,
while they say to me all the day long,
   "Where is your God?"

Then, it seems that the Psalmist slips, even though he views God as 'his rock,' a place of protection from one's enemies. Yes, he now asks, "Why have you forgotten me?" Yes, the Psalmist was allowed to remain in his circumstances of sadness, feeling depressed, as his enemies took pleasure in what appeared to be a victory. The psalmist speaks of himself as being criticized in an unbearable way. So malicious was the mockery and disdain that it could be likened 'as with a deadly wound in his bones.' However, the Levite again comes to himself with self-talk, challenging his irrational thinking with rational thinking.

Wait for God

Psalm 42:11 English Standard Version (ESV)

¹¹ Why are you cast down, O my soul,
 and why are you in turmoil within me?
Hope in God; for I shall again praise him,
 my salvation and my God.

It is not the troubles of the Psalmist, which actually caused him to feel bad. It is what he told himself that contributed to how he felt. Self-talk is what we tell ourselves in our thoughts. In fact, self-talk is the words we tell ourselves about people, self, experiences, life in general, God, the future, the past, the present; it is specifically all the words we say to ourselves all the time. Destructive self-talk, even subconsciously, can be very harmful to our mood: causing mood slumps, our self-worth plummeting, our body feeling sluggish, our will to accomplish even the smallest of things is not to be realized and our actions defeat us.

Intense negative thinking of the Psalmist led to his feeling forsaken, resulting in painful emotions, and depressive state. However, his thoughts based on a good mood were entirely different from those based on his being upset. Negative thoughts that flooded his mind were the actual contributors of his self-defeating emotions. These very thoughts were what kept the Psalmist sluggish and contributed to his feeling abandoned. Therefore, his thinking was also the key to his relief.

Every time the Psalmist felt down because of his irrational self-talk, he attempted to locate the corresponding negative thought he had to this feeling. It was those thoughts that created his feelings of low self-worth. By offsetting them and replacing them with rational thoughts, he actually changed his mood. The negative thoughts that move through his mind did so with no effort, and were the easiest course to follow, because imperfect human tendencies gave him that way of thinking, a pattern of thinking. However, the Psalmist challenged those irrational thoughts of being forsaken with rational ones, saying that he would hope in God and that he would continue to praise him as in the end God is his salvation, even if that salvation comes in the form of a resurrection.

The centerpiece to it all is our Christlike mine. Our moods, behaviors and body responses result from the way we view things (fleshly or spiritual). It is a proven fact that we cannot experience any event in any way, shape, or form unless we have processed it with our mind first. No event can depress us; it is our perception of that event that will contribute to intense sadness, even depression. If we are only sad over an event, our thoughts will be rational, but if we are depressed or anxious over an event, our thinking will be bent and irrational, distorted and utterly wrong.

If we are to remain rational in our thinking, we need to grasp the fact that God does not always step in when we believe he should, nor is he obligated to do so. As was stated earlier, he has greater issues that need resolving, which have eternal effects for the whole of humankind. There is far more times that when God does not step in, meaning that our relief may come in the hope of the resurrection. However, for his servants that apply his Word in a balanced manner, fully, God is acting in their best interest by way of his inspired, inerrant Word.

CHAPTER 2 Does God Provide Bible Absolutes or Guarantees In This Age of Imperfect Humanity?

Many verses (esp. Proverbs) have caused some difficulty in many churches because they are treated like absolutes or guarantees; if we do **A** we will get **B**. Proverbs are not to be applied in this sense in an imperfect world, with imperfect people. The best phrase that we can put before the proverb is "generally speaking." Let us look at Proverbs 22:6 as our first example, it says, "train up a child in the way he should go; even when he is old he will not depart from it." (ESV) Let us look at a easy version of this, "direct your children onto the right path, and when they are older, they will not leave it." (NLT) Is this an absolute guarantee that, if I raise my children in the best way, when they get older they will not leave it? No. Let us place our phrase in front of it. 'Generally speaking,' if you direct your children onto the right path, and when they are older, they will not leave it.'

Again, we ask, is a Bible verse that promises imperfect humans will receive something in this imperfect age to be interpreted as a universal law? Is it as the ancient law of the Medes and the Persians, which could never be overruled (Esther 8:8)? Is it to be interpreted absolutely, like the laws of thermodynamics, which describe what must always take place? It is apparent when reading proverbs that many of them seem to be less than absolute in their applicability. Let us look at a few more examples,

They Sound Like Absolutes

Proverbs 1:33 (New Living Translation)

33 But all who listen to me will live in peace, untroubled by fear of harm."

Is it not true, even some of the most spiritual people we know, have suffered a lack of peace in war-torn countries, or have had trouble in a bad neighborhood, as they fearfully walk to the store, or get in and out of their car, even walk out on their front porch? Was not Stephen of the first century a very spiritual Christian, and was he not martyred?

Proverbs 3:9-10 (New Living Translation)

9 Honor the Lord with your wealth and with the best part of everything you produce. 10 Then he will fill your barns with grain, and your vats will overflow with good wine.

Have not many good Christians given much monetarily as well as their time to the congregation out of their heart over the years, and yet suffered financial disaster during an economic downturn?

Matthew 6:30-33 English Standard Version (ESV)

³⁰ But if God so clothes the grass of the field, which today is alive and tomorrow is thrown into the oven, will he not much more clothe you, O you of little faith? ³¹ Therefore do not be anxious, saying, 'What shall we eat?' or 'What shall we drink?' or 'What shall we wear?' ³² For the Gentiles seek after all these things, and your heavenly Father knows that you need them all. ³³ But seek first the kingdom of God and his righteousness, and all these things will be added to you.

Have not faithful Christians gone hungry, even starved to death? Do not tens of thousands of Christian Children go to bed hungry every night around the world? Are not many Christian homes in this world lacking water? Do not many thousands of Christian families live in rundown homes, having only dirty clothes and in some cases any shoes?

Proverbs 10:3-4 (New Living Translation)

³ The Lord will not let the godly go hungry, but he refuses to satisfy the craving of the wicked.

Are there not many godly Christians going to bed hungry each night?

⁴ Lazy people are soon poor; hard workers get rich.

Are there not poor Christians, who work hard at minimum wage jobs; while there are rich wicked people, who have never worked a day in their life? (See Psalm 73)

Proverbs 13:21 (New Living Translation)

²¹ Trouble chases sinners, while blessings reward the righteous.

Do we measure one's righteous by who is the most blessed? Are all righteous people rich?

Proverbs 17:2 (New Living Translation)

² A wise servant will rule over the master's disgraceful son and will share the inheritance of the master's children.

Are there not rich wicked people?

If We Do "A," i.e., Apply God's Word Correctly We Will, Generally Speaking, Get "B"

It is obvious that none of the above verses and many thousand more within Scripture are absolutes. However, if we follow the rule and place "generally speaking" before the proverb and other verses that appear to be absolutes or guarantees, it will be what the author meant. Generally speaking,

- all who listen to the principles of God, will have peace, untroubled by harm.

- Keeping physically clean contributes to good health. (Deuteronomy 23:12-13)

- God's servants must always speak the truth. (Ephesians 4:25) Sex before marriage, adultery, bestiality, incest, and homosexuality are all serious sins against God. (Leviticus 18:6; Romans 1:26, 27; 1 Corinthians 6:9-10)

- Christians must avoid lying. (Proverbs 6:16-19; Colossians 3:9, 10)

- They do not take part in any kind of gambling. (Ephesians 5:3-5)

- In addition, Christians do not steal.

- Additionally, they do not knowingly buy property that they know to be stolen, nor do they take things without the owner's permission. (Exodus 20:15; Ephesians 4:28)

- Christians have learned to control their anger, as uncontrolled anger can lead to acts of violence. (Genesis 4:5-8)
- Christians know that God does not accept a person that is violent, or even loves violence as His friend. (Psalm 11:5; Proverbs 22:24, 25)

Christians do not take revenge or to return evil for the bad things that others might do to us. (Proverbs 24:29; Romans 12:17-21) There is nothing in the Bible that prohibits drinking alcoholic beverages. (Psalm 104:15; 1 Timothy 5:23) However, heavy drinking and drunkenness are condemned. (1 Corinthians 5:11-13; 1 Timothy 3:8) A person, who consumes too much alcohol will more than likely ruin their health and upset their family. Moreover, it will decrease one's spiritual thinking ability, causing them to give into temptations. (Proverbs 23:20, 21, 29-35)

CHAPTER 3 Are Miracles Still Happening Today?

A writer from *Faith Talk Ministries* writes online, "I was sitting on the balcony, of an Ocean Front Condo in Hawaii, when a thought popped into my mind. The thought was, 'Is God still doing miracles like the ones he did in the Bible?' My wife called me so that we could go and eat. As we were driving down Front Street, in downtown Lahaina, I saw the Bubba Gump Shrimp Company restaurant on the right hand side. I asked my wife if she wanted to eat there. She said, 'Yes' and we went in. The waitress sat us on the side overlooking the ocean. The waitress then took our drink order and left. Actually, it was on my birthday May 7th. I turned around and saw a picture on the wall that said, 'Miracles happen everyday; some people don't think so, but they do.' I was blown away! God had answered my thought from a picture on the wall. Brace yourself! That was a miracle in itself. Some of you maybe saying, 'That was a coincidence!'"[3] This author will go a step further; I do not believe it happened at all. The conclusion of this Faith Talk Ministries writer,

---

[3] http://tiny.cc/8v0ewx

The answer to the question, "Do miracles still happen today," is; Yes. Miracles happen everyday, all day long. God still has a covenant with his children. God still blesses marriage. God still wants to show unbelievers that he is real and that he loves them. The church is still praying and believing God for miracles. God still wants to show us his glory. God told me just the other day; "Behold, I will do a new thing... shall you not see it spring forth?" God still loves us. In fact, Paul said, "For I am persuaded, that neither death, nor life, nor angels, nor principalities, nor powers, nor things present, nor things to come, Nor height, nor depth, nor any other creature, shall be able to separate us from the love of God, which is in Christ Jesus our Lord." (Romans 8:38-39) I challenge everyone who is reading this blog to open your spiritual eyes and watch God do miracles that will blow your natural mind and take you on the journey of your life. I can tell you from experience... there is never a boring day with God. He is a Father that loves to give his children good gifts.[4]

On the question of Does God do miracles today, **compellingtruth.org** offers us a balanced answer.

> Many miracles took place during the times of both Moses and Elijah/Elisha in the Old Testament. The Gospels also record at least 35 miracles by Jesus, while the New Testament records many others that took place at the hands of His disciples. Yet often we do not experience similar miracles today. Does God still perform miracles? Why do the miracles of our times seem unlike the miracles of Bible times?
>
> The answer lies in the purpose of God's miracles. Miracles were performed to authenticate the work of the one performing them. For example, in Acts 2:22 Peter preached, "Men of Israel, hear these words: Jesus of Nazareth, a man attested to you by God with mighty works and wonders and signs that God did through him in your midst, as you yourselves know."

---

[4] IBID

The same was true of the apostles, as 2 Corinthians 12:12 notes, "The signs of a true apostle were performed among you with utmost patience, with signs and wonders and mighty works." Hebrews 2:4 confirms, "while God also bore witness by signs and wonders and various miracles and by gifts of the Holy Spirit distributed according to his will."

These miracles, along with the resurrection of Jesus, the greatest miracle of all, have been recorded for our benefit. God does not need to perform miracles in the same way today. As Jesus taught on one occasion, "If they do not hear Moses and the Prophets, neither will they be convinced if someone should rise from the dead." (Luke 16:31)

In addition, the miracles recorded in the Bible were recorded because they were extraordinary. While those miracles in Scripture are extremely important, they certainly would not have occurred every day. Much of the lives of those in the Bible would have been ordinary, though God was continually at work in the lives of His people and within the early church, just as He is today.

That said, this does not mean God is done performing miracles. By definition, a miracle is something that occurs that is beyond natural explanation. In some parts of the world, accounts are given of people who have had dreams about Jesus and wake up and pray to become a Christian, despite living in an area with no missionary activity and never hearing the teachings of the Bible. In other situations, God has worked through changes of weather or the perfect timing of circumstances in the lives of a person to bring forth an outcome that is part of His perfect will.

God does still perform miracles. However, He does not need to duplicate the actions He has already performed that are available for us to read in the Bible. Instead, we are called to study His Word (2 Timothy 3:16-17) and apply its wisdom and teachings in our lives today.

Perhaps the best advice regarding the miracles of the Bible was given near the end of John's Gospel. After years of following Jesus, he wrote, "Now Jesus did many other signs in the presence of the disciples, which are not written in this book; but these are written so that you may believe that Jesus is the Christ, the Son of God, and that by believing you may have life in his name" (John 20:30-31). The goal of miracles is ultimately for us to believe in Jesus and to live for Him each day.[5]

It should be stated that this author does not deny that God has performed miracles since the days of the New Testament, up unto this very day, and will do so until the return of Christ. However, they are not the same and in the same way, for the same prose, nor to the same extent as certain times within Scriptures. Many of the above quoted points will be expounded on throughout this chapter and others.

Judging Your Own Case

An Apparition in an expanded sense is an appearance of a supposed ghost or something ghostly, but here it is used in the sense of an appearance of Mary. "A Marian apparition is a

---

[5] http://tiny.cc/l50ewx

supernatural appearance by the Blessed Virgin Mary. The figure is often named after the town where it is reported, or on the sobriquet given to Mary on the occasion of the apparition. They have been interpreted in religious terms as theophanies."[6] What are the criteria for evaluating these apparitions of Mary?

The steps of the investigation are mandated as follows: An initial evaluation of the facts of the alleged event, based on both positive and negative criteria:

Positive Criteria

1. moral certainty (the certainty required to act morally in a situation of doubt) or at least great probability as to the existence of a private revelation at the end of a serious investigation into the case

2. evaluation of the personal qualities of the person in question (mental balance, honesty, moral life, sincerity, obedience to Church authority, willingness to practice faith in the normal way, etc.)

3. evaluation of the content of the revelations themselves (that they do not

---

[6] http://en.wikipedia.org/wiki/Marian_apparition

disagree with faith and morals of the Church, freedom from theological errors)

4. the revelation results in healthy devotion and spiritual fruits in people's lives (greater prayer, greater conversion of heart, works of charity that result, etc.)

Negative Criteria

1. glaring errors in regard to the facts
2. doctrinal errors attributed to God, the Blessed Virgin Mary, or to the Holy Spirit in how they appear
3. any pursuit of financial gain in relation to the alleged event
4. gravely immoral acts committed by the person or those associated with the person at the time of the event
5. psychological disorders or tendencies on the part of the person or persons associated

After this initial investigation, if the occurrence meets the criteria, positive and negative, an initial cautionary permission can be granted that states: "for the moment, there is nothing opposed to it". This permits public participation in the devotion concerning the alleged apparition.[7]

Our Lady of the Pillar: In the year AD 39, according to tradition, the Virgin Mary appeared to Saint James the Great, in Zaragoza, Spain. The vision is now called Our Lady of the Pillar and is the only reported Marian apparition before her Assumption. The Basilica of Our Lady of the Pillar was built in Zaragoza, Spain and a key piece of Roman Catholic Marian art, the statue of Our Lady of the Pillar, refers to this apparition.[8]

Our Lady of Lourdes: In 1858 Saint Bernadette Soubirous was a 14-year-old shepherd girl who lived near the town of Lourdes in France. Bernadette Soubirous was out gathering firewood in the countryside. She reported a vision of a miraculous Lady who identified Herself as "the Immaculate Conception" in subsequent visions.

Our Lady of Banneux: A young child, Mariette Beco a native of Banneux, Belgium in the 1930s, reported the apparitions of Our Lady of Banneux. They are also known as the Virgin of the Poor. The Roman Catholic Church

---

[7] IBID

[8] IBID

approved the apparitions in 1949.[9] Beco reported eight visions of the Blessed Virgin Mary between January 15 and March 2, 1933. She reported seeing a Lady in White who declared herself the *Virgin of the Poor* and told her: "Believe in me and I will believe in you". In one vision, the Lady reportedly asked Mariette to drink from a small spring and later said that the spring was for healing. Over time, the site drew pilgrims. Today, the small spring yields about 2,000 gallons of water a day with many reports of miraculous healings.[10]

One can see the problem of investigating your own claims. Those who made claims of seeing Mary were in harmony with the model established by the church. Are we surprised to find that these apparitions approved by the Catholic Church confirm the churches traditions and doctrines exclusively? Thus, we ask ourselves, are the supposed miracles and apparitions actually signs from heaven that prove the truth, accuracy and reliability of the Catholic Church's teachings? It is self-defeating in that it takes its own authority as to whether

---

[9] Michael Freze, 1993, *Voices, Visions, and Apparitions*, OSV Publishing

[10] Memorare http://www.memorare.com/mary/app1933.html

apparitions and related miracles come from God or not; i.e., it is its own judge. All good Roman Catholics believe that the popes throughout history were infallible and cannot err or make a mistake when issuing decrees on faith and morals. Well, let us judge the supreme judges of the Roman Catholic Church. If the men that follow are without error and can forgive sins, it does not agree or is not consistent with Scripture.

A Brief Papal History

Stephen VI was Pope from 896 to 897. Fueled by his anger with Pope Formosus, his predecessor, he exhumed Formosus's rotting corpse and put "him" on trial, in the so-called "Cadaver Synod" in January 897.

With the corpse propped up on a throne, a deacon was appointed to answer for the deceased pontiff, who was condemned for performing the functions of a bishop when he had been deposed and for receiving the pontificate while he was the bishop of Porto, among other revived charges that had been leveled against Formosus in the strife during the pontificate of John VIII.

The corpse was found guilty, stripped of its sacred vestments, deprived of three fingers of its right hand (the blessing fingers), clad in the garb of a layman, and quickly buried; it was then re-exhumed and thrown in the Tiber. All ordinations performed by Formosus were annulled.

The trial excited a tumult. Though the instigators of the deed may actually have been Formosus' enemies of the House of Spoleto (notably Guy IV of Spoleto), who had recovered their authority in Rome at the beginning of 897 by renouncing their broader claims in central Italy, the scandal ended in Stephen's imprisonment and his death by strangling that summer.[11]

Benedict IX was Pope from 1032 to 1044, again in 1045, and finally from 1047 to 1048, the only man to have served as Pope for three discontinuous periods, and one of the most controversial Popes of all time. Benedict gave up his papacy for the first time in exchange for a large sum of money in 1044. He returned in 1045 to depose his replacement and reigned for one month, after which he left again, possibly to marry, and sold the papacy for a second time, to his Godfather (possibly for over 650 kg /1450 lb of gold). Two years later,

---

[11] http://en.wikipedia.org/wiki/Pope_Stephen_VI

Benedict retook Rome and reigned for an additional one year, until 1048. Poppo of Brixen (later to become Pope Damascus II) eventually forced him out of Rome. Benedict's place and date of death are unknown, but some speculate that he made further attempts to regain the Papal Throne. St. Peter Damian described him as "feasting on immorality" and "a demon from hell in the disguise of a priest" in the Liber Gomorrhianus, a treatise on papal corruption and sex that accused Benedict IX of routine homosexuality and bestiality.[12]

Sergius III was Pope from 897 to 911, and has been the only pope known to have ordered the murder of another pope and the only known to have fathered an illegitimate son who later became pope; his pontificate has been described as "dismal and disgraceful." The pontificate of Sergius III was remarkable for the rise of what papal historians call a "pornocracy," or rule of the harlots, a reversal of the natural order as they saw it, according to Liber pontificalis and a later chronicler who was also biased against Sergius III. This "pornocracy" was an age with women in power: Theodora, whom Liutprand characterized as a "shameless whore... [who] exercised power on the Roman

---

[12] http://en.wikipedia.org/wiki/Pope_Benedict_IX

citizenry like a man" and her daughter Marozia, the mother of Pope John XI (931–935) and reputed to be the mistress of Sergius III.[13]

John XII was Pope from 955 to 964. On 963, Holy Roman Emperor Otto I summoned a council, levelling charges that John had ordained a deacon in a stable, consecrated a 10-year-old boy as bishop of Todi, converted the Lateran Palace into a brothel, raped female pilgrims in St. Peter's, stolen church offerings, drank toasts to the devil, and invoked the aid of Jove, Venus, and other pagan gods when playing dice. He was deposed, but returned as pope when Otto left Rome, maiming and mutilating all who had opposed him. On 964, he was apparently beaten by the husband of a woman with which he was having an affair, dying three days later without receiving confession or the sacraments.[14]

Leo X was Pope from 1513 to his death in 1521. He is known primarily for the sale of indulgences to reconstruct St. Peter's Basilica and his challenging of Martin Luther's 95 theses.

---

[13] http://en.wikipedia.org/wiki/Pope_Sergius_III

[14] http://en.wikipedia.org/wiki/Pope_John_XII

According to Alexandre Dumas, "under his pontificate, Christianity assumed a pagan character, which, passing from art into manners, gives to this epoch a strange complexion. Crimes for the moment disappeared, to give place to vices; but to charming vices, vices in good taste, such as those indulged in by Alcibiades and sung by Catullus." When he became Pope, Leo X is reported to have said to his brother Giuliano: "Since God has given us the papacy, let us enjoy it."

His extravagance offended not only people like Martin Luther, but also some cardinals, who, led by Alfonso Petrucci of Siena, plotted an assassination attempt. Eventually, Pope Leo found out who these people were, and had them followed. The conspirators died of "food poisoning." Some people argue that Leo X and his followers simply concocted the assassination charges in a moneymaking scheme to collect fines from the various wealthy cardinals Leo X detested.[15]

Alexander VI was Pope from 1492 to 1503. He is the most controversial of the secular popes of the Renaissance, and his surname (Italianized as Borgia) became a

---

[15] http://en.wikipedia.org/wiki/Pope_Leo_X

byword for the debased standards of the papacy of that era. Originally Cardinal Borgia from Spain, Pope Alexander's claims to fame were taking over much of Italy by force with the help of his son Cesare (yes, his son), a racy relationship with his daughter Lucrezia (some say her son was his), and his affinity for throwing large parties, bordering on orgies, that usually culminated with little naked boys jumping out of large cakes.[16]

Innocent IV was Pope from 1243 to 1254. Certainly the Inquisition represents the darkest of Roman Church history, and it was Innocent IV who approved the use of torture to extract confessions of heresy. He aggressively applied the principle that "the end justifies the means." It is shocking to learn about the deranged instruments of torture that were used on so many innocent people. One of the most famous people to suffer at the hands of Roman inquisitors was Galileo. The church condemned Galileo for claiming that the earth revolved around the sun.[17]

Urban VI was Pope from 1378 to 1389. He was the first Pope of the Western Schism

---

[16] http://en.wikipedia.org/wiki/Pope_Alexander_VI

[17] http://en.wikipedia.org/wiki/Pope_Innocent_IV

(which ultimately lead to three people claiming the Papal throne at the same time). Once elected, he was prone to outbursts of rage. The cardinals who elected him decided that they had made the wrong decision and they elected a new Pope in his place, so he took the name of Clement VII and started a second Papal court in Avignon, France. Later he would launch a program of violence against those he thought to have been conspiring against him, imprisoning people at will and mistreating them brutally. Later historians have considered seriously that he might have been insane.

The second election threw the Church into turmoil. There had been antipopes, rival claimants to the papacy, before, but most of them had been appointed by various rival factions; in this case, the legitimate leaders of the Church themselves had created both popes. The conflict quickly escalated from a church problem to a diplomatic crisis that divided Europe. Secular leaders had to choose which pope they would recognize. The schism was repaired forty years later when all three of the (then) reigning Popes abdicated together and a successor elected in the person of Pope Martin V.[18]

---

[18] http://en.wikipedia.org/wiki/Pope_Urban_VI

John XV was Pope from 985 to 996. The Pope's venality and nepotism had made him very unpopular with the citizens, as he split the church's finances among his relatives and was described as "covetous of filthy lucre and corrupt in all his acts."[19]

Clement VII was Pope from 1523 to 1534. A member of the powerful Medici family, Clement VII possessed great political and diplomatic skills - but he lacked the understanding of the age necessary to cope with the political and religious changes he faced. His relationship with Emperor Charles V was so bad that, in May 1527, Charles invaded Italy and sacked Rome.

Imprisoned, Clement was forced into a humiliating compromise, which forced him to give up a great deal of secular and religious power. Eventually, Clement became ill and never recovered. He died on September 25, 1534, hated by the people of Rome, who never forgave him for the destruction of 1527.[20]

These wicked men are supposed to be the supreme leader of God's kingdom here on earth, having the authority to forgive sins, are

---

[19] http://en.wikipedia.org/wiki/Pope_John_XV

[20] http://en.wikipedia.org/wiki/Pope_Clement_VII

supposedly infallible, unable to err or make mistakes when issuing decrees on faith and morals. When we examine the facts, it becomes all too clear that the claim of infallibility for the Pope is a complete falsehood intended to deceive trusting people. The Bible has the following to say of religious leaders, who deceive, "For such men are false apostles, deceitful workmen, disguising themselves as apostles of Christ." (2 Cor. 11:13) Jesus warned what would happen if anyone were to blindly follow such men as this, "If the blind lead the blind, both will fall into a pit."—Matthew 15:14.

Alleged Evidence of Miracles

Marie Bernarde "Bernadette" Soubirous (Occitan: Bernadeta Sobirós; 1844–1879) was the firstborn daughter of a miller from Lourdes, France, and is venerated as a Christian mystic and Saint in the Catholic Church.

Soubirous is best known for the Marian apparitions of a "small young lady" who asked for a chapel to be built at the nearby garbage dump of the cave-grotto at Massabielle where apparitions are said to have occurred between 11 February and 16 July 1858. She would later receive recognition when the lady who appeared to her identified herself as the **Immaculate Conception**.

Despite initial skepticism from the Catholic Church, Soubirous's claims were eventually declared "worthy of belief" after a canonical investigation, and the Marian apparition is now known as Our Lady of Lourdes. Since her death, Soubirous's body has apparently remained internally incorrupt, but it is not without blemish; during her third exhumation in 1925, the firm of Pierre Imans made light wax coverings for her face and her hands due to the discoloration that her skin had undergone. These masks were placed on her face and hands before she was moved to her crystal reliquary in June 1925.[21]

The Immaculate Conception, according to the teaching of the Catholic Church, was the conception of the Blessed Virgin Mary in her

---

[21]

http://en.wikipedia.org/wiki/Bernadette_Soubirous

mother's womb free from original sin by virtue of the foreseen merits of her son Jesus Christ.

The Immaculate Conception is commonly confused with the doctrine of the Incarnation and the virgin birth of Jesus, though the two deal with separate subjects. The Catholic Church teaches that Mary was conceived by normal biological means, but her soul was acted upon by God (kept "immaculate") at the time of her conception.[22]

What are we to make of the "Immaculate Conception" of which Bernadette spoke? This is a blatant contradiction of what the Bible teaches. The Bible is quite clear that all of Adam's descendants, except Jesus Christ himself, was brought forth in iniquity, and in sin was conceived, for all have sinned and fall short of the glory of God.' (Ps. 51:5; Rom. 3:23) If Mary was conceived free from original sin, why did she present a sin offering after Jesus was born. (Lev. 12:6; Lu 2:22-24) Moreover, there is not one Scripture, which states that Mary in her mother's womb was free from original sin, to support Catholic doctrine.

---

[22] http://en.wikipedia.org/wiki/Immaculate_Conception

The *New Catholic Encyclopedia* (1967, Vol. VII, pp. 378-381) acknowledges regarding the origin of the belief: " . . . the Immaculate Conception is not taught explicitly in Scripture . . . The earliest Church Fathers regarded Mary as holy but not as absolutely sinless. . . . It is impossible to give a precise date when the belief was held as a matter of faith, but by the 8th or 9th century it seems to have been generally admitted. . . . [In 1854 Pope Pius IX defined the dogma] 'which holds that the most Blessed Virgin Mary was preserved from all stain of original sin in the first instant of her Conception.'" This belief was confirmed by Vatican II (1962-1965).—*The Documents of Vatican II* (New York, 1966), edited by W. M. Abbott, S.J., p. 88.

The Bible itself says, "Well then, sin entered the world through one man [Adam], and through sin death, and thus death has spread through the whole human race because *everyone* has sinned." (Rom. 5:12, Jerusalem Bible) Clearly, the worship of Mary is not biblical; therefore, the apparitions are not from God.

If the apparitions took place, they could be from another source. Jesus said, "For false christs and false prophets will arise and perform great signs and wonders, so as to lead astray, if possible, even the elect." (Matt. 24:24) Jesus performed many miracles in his three and a half years of ministry. He changed water into wine, provided food for crowds numbering into the thousands, healed the sick, raised the dead, and expelled demons. Why did he perform so many miracles? How can we better understand today's miracles?

Within Jesus' life, more than forty Old Testament prophecies were fulfilled, coupled with his teachings, resulted in many believing that he was the long awaited Messiah. For others, I was the miracles, as they reasoned, "When the Christ appears, will he do more signs than this man has done?"–John 7:31.

Purpose of Miracles

What was the purpose behind Jesus' miracles? Deuteronomy 18:15, 18 say that the Messiah would 'be a prophet like Moses.' God goes on to say, "I will put my words in his mouth, and he shall speak to them all that I command him." In order for Moses to be accepted as God's spokesperson, he initially performed many miracles. (Ex. 4:1-9, 30-31) Just as Moses performed many miracles to establish his purpose, Jesus actually performed far more, even raising people from the dead and casting out demons.—Acts 3:22.

We know that Jesus was more than Moses and his authority and power demonstrate such. What Jesus did on a small scale during his three and a half year ministry, will be exceeded in the extreme upon his return. If Jesus was able to feed thousands miraculously with a few loaves and fishes, he will certainly restore this earth to how God had intended it in the beginning of creating it for perfect humanity. (Lu 9:12-17) Therefore, none will ever hunger again. (Ps. 72:16) Moreover, he will not only heal and cure humans, but will also restore them to perfection, so that they will be able to live forever. (Rev. 21:4) Lastly, like with his friend Lazarus and others, Jesus will resurrect millions from the dead. (Lu 7:11-17; 8:40-56; John 5:28, 29; 11:11-44)

The one reason that Jesus was rejected by Jews like Saul (i.e., Paul), was because he did not carry out on a grand scale, the things listed in the Old Testament. For example, it was prophesied of Jesus' coming kingdom, "In the days of those kings the God of heaven will set up a kingdom that shall never be destroyed, nor shall the kingdom be left to another people. It shall break in pieces all these kingdoms and bring them to an end, and it shall stand forever." (Dan 2:44) What those Jews though was going to take place on a larger scale on Jesus' first coming, will be far grandeur at his second coming, for the first time was simply a preview of the things to come.

Miracles were Evidence of Change

The miracles of the Hebrew Scriptures, especially those performed by Moses, served as evidence that the Jews, descendants of faithful Abraham, were God's chose people. (Ex. 19:16-19) A major change was in the offing. The Jews had followed the lead of their religious leaders in the last act of rebellion, resulting in their rejection as his people. The Mosaic Law was being replaced with the law of Christ. This does not mean that no Jew could be received into the newly founded Christian congregation. To the contrary, the next three and half years would be only the Jewish people, who would make up this new way to God. As was the case with Moses, there was to be a sign, miraculous events, this served as evidence to those, whose heart was receptive to the truth that the Son of God had come, had given his life for them, and ascended back to heaven.

This served as evidence that there was a new way to God, i.e., Christ and Christianity.

(Matt. 21:43; 27:51; Rom. 9:6; 11:7) The many miracles by the apostles that followed Jesus' miracles served as evidence that the Christian congregation was the Truth and the Way, not fleshly Israel. (Acts 2:22, 43; 4:29-30; Heb. 2:3-4) Moreover, think of the account where people bring their sick ones in places where Peter's shadow might fall on them as he walked by. On this the Bible states, "They were all healed." (Acts 5:15-16) This begs the question, why are not all the faithful ones healed when they go to these religious shrines.

The Purpose has Been Served

What was the purpose again? The miracles and signs served to establish Jesus as the Son of God, to evidence on a small scale what he will do upon his return on a grandeur scale, and to establish that Christianity was now the Truth and the Way to God, not fleshly Israel. The miraculous gifs served their purpose, so they would "cease." (1 Cor. 13:8-13) There will be more on this later. Miracles does not evidence true Christianity, it is doing the will of the Father that evidences whether one is a true Christian or a denomination is true Christianity. Jesus foretold,

Matthew 7:21-23 English Standard Version (ESV)

²¹ "Not everyone who says to me, 'Lord, Lord,' will enter the kingdom of heaven, but the one who **does the will of my Father** who is in heaven. ²² On that day **many will say** to me, 'Lord, Lord, **did we not prophesy** in your name, and **cast out demons** in your name, and do **many mighty works** in your name?' ²³ And then will I declare to them, 'I never knew you; depart from me, you workers of lawlessness.'

The Mark of True Christianity

Jesus told us how we can identify his true disciples, when he said, 'by their fruit you will recognize them.' Jesus gives us the gist of his point, "A good tree cannot produce bad fruit, nor can a bad tree produce good fruit." (Matt. 7:16-20) One identifying fruit is **the teachings** upon which the denomination is based. Are the teachings based on God's Word or the traditions of men? (2 Tim. 3:16; Mark 7:7) Another identifying fruit would be whether they are evidencing truth **faith in Christ**. (John 3:36; Ps. 2:6-8; Jam. 2:26) Is it ritualistic or a formality, or is it a **way of life**. (Isa. 1:15-17; 1 Cor. 5:9-13; Eph. 5:3-5; Gal. 5:22-23) Jesus mentions yet another fruit when he said, "By this all people will know that you are my disciples, if you have love for one another." (John 13:35) Is it and its members a part of the world? (John 15:19; Jam 1:27; 4:4; 1 John 2:15-17) Are the true Christians carrying out the witnessing and evangelism work that Jesus assigned? (Matt 24:14; 28:19-20; Ac 1:8) Thus, it follows that miracles are no longer need as evidence that Christianity is the Truth and the Way, but rather other markers are needed to identify which of the more than 41,000 denominations are the Truth and the Way.

Thus, miracles were not to serve as an identifying marker forever. Therefore, our faith should not be based on a plethora of miracles taking place today. Rather, it should be grounded on the truths found in the Word of God. The focus needs to be on the sharing of God's Word in our communities and living in harmony with that Word. Our complete trust must be placed in the Father, the Son and the provision of the Holy Spirit. Peter tells us, "there is salvation in no one else, for there is no other name under heaven given among men by which we must be saved."–Acts 4:12

CHAPTER 4 Is Faith Healing Scriptural

Really, there are two different thoughts when it comes to faith healing: (1) the scandalous evangelist standing on stage healing some cripple, and (2) some person living through or receiver from some tragic illness or accident. We picture the little girl in the wheelchair in an audience that can move nothing but her eyes, as the preacher is walking back and forth on the stage ranting to the point of spit flying everywhere. Soon some attendant wheels the little girl onto the stage, where the priest shakes her, screaming to God, speaking in some unknown language (gibberish), in the end the girl starts to move, and in minutes, she is able to get up out of the chair and walk, to the joy and teas of thousands in the audience.

Then, thousands of miles away, there is another little girl critically ill at home under hospice care. She has an inoperable brain tumor. She is in the last days of her life. Her church prays one night through the entire night, only to find the next morning the girl is taken back to the hospital because she has appeared to of made a turnaround. When they do a brain scan, the doctors find no traces of a tumor; it is as though she never had one in the first place. We can hear this hypothetical little girls words, as her lips tremble through the tears, "The doctors were so stunned and could not believe it," she said through the tears. "I was supposed to be dead within the 48-hours, I was literally on death's door. Then it happened, I started to feel myself literally come back to life as it were. I should not even be alive, but God has chosen to save me." Imagine the joy of those church members, the families of both children. Both are being hailed as a miracle from God.

What is Faith Healing?

The faith healers in the West, i.e., countries of Europe and North and South America, take place by evangelists or ministers of different denominations, but more so with those of the charismatic movement (e.g., Pentecostals). The faith healers claim that they are carrying out a similar work of Jesus Christ and his apostles, having the power of God move through them.

Of course, there are the "healers" from religions outside of Christianity, which is more in line with voodoo priests, witch doctors, medicine men and the like. These believe that evil spirits cause sickness and they carry out ceremonies to drive the evil spirits away. There are what is known as "psychic surgeons" as well, who literally carry out psychic surgeries" in places such as the Philippines. Then, there are those that claim that miraculous healings are from the natural forces that surround us and have nothing to do with any religion. We only mention these in passing, because this book is dealing with Christians, and claims of what appears to be miraculous faith healing within Christianity.

Does Faith Healing Work?

Many times, we have seen or heard a doctor on the news saying that it is a miracle that so and so is alive, and they have no explanation as to why. If asked specifically about their use of the word "miracle," they usually are not attributing it to God, but rather as an event that appears to be contrary to the laws of nature, which the religious regarded as an act of God. The doctor generally uses the word as a figure of speech. One thing is for certain; the faith part of faith healing is really at play here and not in the way one might think. We cannot say for certain nor can we prove that any person's recovery is because God intervened, because similar recoveries have taken place with atheists and even those of the darker side of things, like Wiccans.

What we know about the human mind is so minuscule that it cannot even be expressed accurately. What we do know or think we know is like a piece of sand out of all the beaches of sand in the world, and it amazing and astounding, which could fill thousands of books. Now, try to imagine what we do not know. The effect of the mind on the body's health is similarly unknown. How diseases react to the mind is not fully understood either. However, all medical professionals will tell you that if the patient has the attitude that they are going to die and that they could never beat their disease, it takes place far, far faster than those that see the victory over the disease and fight as if they are in an Olympic game. Now, couple that latter person with the mindset of one with great faith in God. The real miracle here is the brain and the mind, a gift from God.

Is There Any Harm In Believing in Faith Healing?

If a person is charismatic in their belief, believing that whatever happens is God's will, or worse still that God will help the faithful regardless. While this positive attitude may help the body to stay the course for a time, this person might not see the need for a doctor. Truly, that question lies before us as well. If

God is going to heal the person regardless, why even see a doctor? What is the purpose? On the belief that the person living or dying is predestined, and nothing can change the outcome, why see a doctor? This author is personally aware of a person who did not see a doctor for her cancer, and she eventually dies a horrific death, which some confused Christian minds would say that was God's will. However, the cancer she had could have been easily beaten through medical technology. What many ultra-religious persons are not aware of; medical science is a gift from God as well. The knowledge and understanding that enables doctors to cure and save people comes from the human mind, which God created, and even in imperfection, we have the capacity to accomplish much.

Some Similarities Cannot Be Ignored

During faith healing services or healing prayers by the church for the sick, it is noteworthy that some "speak in tongues," with some even falling into a trancelike state, where they cannot move, but say they were ware of everything happening. If we were to get the complete picture in many of these services, it would be very similar to the fits and trances, which include the other religious healers, i.e., the voodoo priests and witch doctors. While the psychic healers believe that their healings are not like that of religions, yet the procedures and experiences are very similar to the end. The procedures ad experiences are very similar to Spiritism, which come from many of the ancient oriental religions. Let us take a moment and consider what the procedure and experiences were like when Jesus and his apostles healed.

Jesus Heals

When Jesus healed, we find not charismatic jumping around, emotionalism, no speaking in tongues, no rants and ravings, no fits and trances, and no emotional sermons beforehand. In fact, when Jesus healed someone there was no big scene, it was quite informal. The one who was sick might touch Jesus, or Jesus might touch him, but there was no shaking him or smacking him in the forehead. At times, Jesus just lovingly spoke to the person, and they were healed.—Matthew 8:14-15; Luke 8:43-48; 17:12-19.

When Jesus healed physical illness, the cure was not by mental factors of mind and body. On one Sabbath, Jesus entered the synagogue and was teaching, and a man was there whose right hand was withered. Jesus said him,

"Stretch out your hand." He did so, and his hand was restored. Psychosomatic healing cannot cure a withered hand. Certainly, there is no psychosomatic healing when raising the dead, which Jesus did with Lazarus, who had been dead for four days. (Matt. 4:23; Luke 6:6-11; 8:49-56) There was not one person who simply made small improvements in their healing; he never failed, but rather Jesus fully healed every disease and every affliction. We never hear of words like "disappointment" or "deception" in connection with Jesus' healings. Even Jesus' enemies, the Jewish religious leaders complained, "What are we to do? For this man performs many signs." (John 11:47-48) Do we notice the differences?

If faith healers heal any today, in their connection with spiritistic procedures and experiences, we must ask what the source of this power is. The Bible made the following warning, which I believe we need to take to heart.

Deuteronomy 18:10-11 English Standard Version (ESV)

[10] There shall not be found among you anyone who burns his son or his daughter as an offering, anyone who practices divination or tells fortunes or interprets omens, or a

sorcerer [11] or a charmer or a medium or a necromancer or one who inquires of the dead,

The purpose of this publication is to protect the modern day Christian from being contaminated by demonic spirit forces, which are under the leadership of Satan himself, seeking to stumble any in their walk with God. When we think of the modern day faith healers and their practices that very much resemble spiritistic practices, are in no way similar to those carried out by Jesus Christ. The common sense of seeing through these fraudulent ones is further appreciated when we realize the purpose of Jesus' healing was completed in the first century and will not be seen again until his second coming.

What Was the Purpose of Jesus' Healing?

1 Timothy 5:23 English Standard Version (ESV)

[23] (No longer drink only water, but use a little wine for the sake of your stomach and your frequent ailments.)

Here we see the Paul's closest traveling companion and friend, Timothy was suffering from some frequent stomach ailment. Paul told Timothy, "Do not be hasty in the laying on of hands," but rather to use a common medical treatment. It should be noted that the early Christians who personally witnessed actual healings, even the raising of others from the dead by Jesus and the apostles, did not view the gift of healing as some form of therapy. Moreover, they were not given the commission to care for the physical well-being of humanity.

They had another commission, one that Jesus carried out and assigned to every Christian just before his ascension, to proclaim the gospel, to teach and to make disciples. Jesus told Pontius Pilate the purpose of his coming to earth. He said, "For this purpose I was born and for this purpose I have come into the world, to bear witness to the truth. Everyone who is of the truth listens to my voice."–John 18:37.

Why then did Jesus and the apostles heal people in the first-century? The healings and other miracles served as a sign. The Jewish people had been God's chosen people for 1,500-years, and now God was choosing another way for humankind to approach him, i.e., Christianity. Thus, the healings and other miracles were a sign that Christianity was now the Way and the Truth. The apostle Paul wrote,[23]

Hebrews 2:3-4 English Standard Version (ESV)

³ how shall we escape if we neglect such a great salvation? It was declared at first by the Lord, and it was attested to us by those who heard, ⁴ while **God also <u>bore witness</u> by <u>signs</u> and <u>wonders</u> and various <u>miracles</u>** and by gifts of the Holy Spirit distributed according to his will.

The primary focus of first-century Christianity was not miracles but the bearing witness to Jesus Christ. This is why Christianity grew from five hundred disciples in 33 C.E. to over one million by 125 C.E., less that one hundred years later. The miracles simply were the evident demonstration to the Jews that God had chosen another course of drawing close to him. After the Christian congregation, was well grounded in the first-century, the gifts of the spirit, which included healing were no longer needed. (1 Cor. 12:27–13:8) What about those claiming to perform miracles today in Jesus name?

---

[23] http://www.christianpublishers.org/the-jews-chosen-people

Matthew 7:21-23 English Standard Version (ESV)

²¹ "Not everyone who says to me, 'Lord, Lord,' will enter the kingdom of heaven, but **the one <u>who does</u> <u>the will</u> of my Father** who is in heaven. ²² On that day many will say to me, 'Lord, Lord, **did we not** prophesy in your name, and cast out demons in your name, and **do many mighty works** in your name?' ²³ And then will I declare to them, 'I never knew you; depart from me, you workers of lawlessness.'

Rather, here is where Jesus said the work of the Christian would lie,

Matthew 24:14 English Standard Version (ESV)

¹⁴ And this gospel of the kingdom will be proclaimed throughout the whole world as a testimony to all nations, and then the end will come.

Matthew 28:19-20 English Standard Version (ESV)

¹⁹ Go therefore and make disciples of all nations, baptizing them in the name of the Father and of the Son and of the Holy Spirit, ²⁰ teaching them to observe all that I have

commanded you. And behold, I am with you always, to the end of the age."

When the Bible was completed, thirty-nine books of the Old Testament and twenty-seven books of the New Testament, the Christian had everything they needed to get them to Jesus second coming. When we think of the videos of the Pentecostal Church and other Charismatic groups, and the jumping around, body jerking, speaking in tongues, trances, and faith healing, we must realize that this showy display of oneself is not for God. In fact, the apostle Paul identified the speaking in tongues (not ecstatic speech, gibberish, but rather speaking a foreign language), with the babyhood of Christianity. After mentioning that speaking in tongues would cease, Paul wrote, "When I was a child, I spoke like a child, I thought like a child, I reasoned like a child. When I became a man, I gave up childish ways." According to Paul's own words, the historical evidence of the book of Acts and second century writers, speaking in tongues passed away. (1 Cor. 13:8-11) Please see [Chapter 5 Is Speaking in Tongues Evidence of True Christianity?](#)

Therefore, these showy displays of oneself must come from a different source than the "gifts of the spirit" in the first-century. The source is spiritistic, not the Spirit of God. Thus, we need to heed the warning of the apostle John, "Beloved, do not believe every spirit, but test the spirits to see whether they are from God, for many false prophets have gone out into the world."–1 John 4:1.

God's Word is Alive

Hebrews 4:12 English Standard Version (ESV)

¹² For the word of God is living and active, sharper than any two-edged sword, piercing to the division of soul and of spirit, of joints and of marrow, and discerning the thoughts and intentions of the heart.

Nowhere in Scripture will we find a promise that we will receive an instant relief from sickness.[24] However, while the Bible is not a medical journal, it does offer extensive help on health matters. People who obeyed the Bible's guidance on physical and moral cleanness were able to avoid diseases long before science ever had knowledge of germs. Then, if we were to apply the counsel on envy, jealousy and fits of anger, we would avoid many stress-related illnesses, including strokes

---

[24] See Chapter 2 Does God Provide Bible Absolutes or Guarantees In This Age of Imperfect Humanity?

and heart attacks.—Proverbs 14:29, 30; 2 Corinthians 7:1; Galatians 5:19-23.

If we are not anxious but rely fully on God's Word in the times of sickness; we can have,

Philippians 4:6-7 English Standard Version (ESV)

⁶ do not be anxious about anything, but in everything by prayer and supplication with thanksgiving let your requests be made known to God. ⁷ And **the peace of God, which surpasses all understanding**, will **guard your hearts and your minds** in Christ Jesus.

One day soon, Jesus will remove the selfish, violent, wicked humankind and these oppressive human governments, to rule the earth for a thousand years. The apostle Peter said that Jesus' miracles were "mighty works and wonders and signs." (Acts 2:22) They were "signs" of the truths that Jesus gave us, and they were "wonders"[25] of what God will do for

---

[25] The Greek word rendered "wonders" is *teras*, has the sense of any amazing or wonderful occurrence; especially used of something seemingly preternatural, i.e., exceeding what is normal in nature. (Bible Sense Lexicon by Logos) *Teras* appeals to the imagination, manifested as divine operations. W. E. Vine, Merrill F. Unger, and William White Jr., Vine's *Complete Expository Dictionary*

humanity when Jesus' kingdom carries out the will and purposes of the Father to be done in all the earth. Envision the healing and restoration work that will occur.

Moreover, while there is a heavenly hope, there is also another hope,

The New Earth: The Earthly Hope

In the O[ld] T[estament] the kingdom of God is usually described in terms of a redeemed earth; this is especially clear in the book of Isaiah, where the final state of the universe is already called new heavens and a new earth (65:17; 66:22) The nature of this renewal was perceived only very dimly by OT authors, but they did express the belief that a humans ultimate destiny is an earthly one.[26] This vision is clarified in the N[ew] T[estament]. Jesus speaks of the "renewal" of the world (Matt

---

of Old and New Testament Words (Nashville, TN: T. Nelson, 1996), 682.

[26] It is unwise to speak of the written Word of God as if it were of human origin, saying 'OT authors express the belief,' when what was written is the meaning and message of what God wanted to convey by means of the human author.

19:28), Peter of the restoration of all things (Acts 3:21). Paul writes that the universe will be redeemed by God from its current state of bondage (Rom. 8:18-21). This is confirmed by Peter, who describes the new heavens and the new earth as the Christian's hope (2 Pet. 3:13). Finally, the book of Revelation includes a glorious vision of the end of the present universe and the creation of a new universe, full of righteousness and the presence of God. The vision is confirmed by God in the awesome declaration: "I am making everything new!" (Rev. 21:1-8).

The new heavens and the new earth will be the renewed creation that will fulfill the purpose for which God created the universe. It will be characterized by the complete rule of God and by the full realization of the final goal of redemption: "Now the dwelling of God is with men" (Rev. 21:3).

The fact that the universe will be created anew[27] shows that God's goals for humans is not an ethereal [heavenly] and disembodied existence, but a bodily existence on a perfected earth. The scene of the beatific vision is the new earth. The spiritual does not exclude the created order and will be fully realized only within a perfected creation. (Elwell 2001, 828-29)

God created the earth to be inhabited, to be filled with perfect humans, who are over the animals, and under the sovereignty of God. (Gen. 1:28; 2:8, 15; Ps. 104:5; 115:16; Eccl. 1:4) Sin did not dissuade God from his plans (Isa. 45:18); on the contrary, he has saved redeemable humankind by Jesus' ransom sacrifice. It seems that the Bible offers two hopes to redeemed humans, **(1) a heavenly hope**, or **(2) an earthly hope**. It also seems that those with the heavenly hope are limited in number, and are going to heaven to rule with Christ as kings, priests, and judges either **on** the earth or **over** the earth from heaven. In addition, it seems that those with the earthly

---

[27] Create anew does not mean a complete destruction followed by a re-creation, but instead a renewal of the present universe.

hope are going to receive eternal life here on a renewed earth as originally intended. The book of Revelation describes this future healing,

Revelation 21:4-5 English Standard Version (ESV)

⁴ He will wipe away every tear from their eyes, and death shall be no more, neither shall there be mourning, nor crying, nor pain anymore, for the former things have passed away."

⁵ And he who was seated on the throne said, "Behold, I am making all things new." Also he said, "Write this down, for these words are trustworthy and true."

What we have learned within this publication thus far is that God performed miracles in the past, but they were the exception to the rule. Even during the 4,000 years of biblical times, miracles were not the norm, and many times hundreds of years passed without any record of miracles taking place. When we see a cluster of miracles taking place within Scripture, it was a transitional period, such as,

- Abraham being called to a new land,
- Moses leading the Israelites out of Egypt and slavery,

- prophets warning of a coming punishment for northern Israel and southern Judah,
- and Jesus establishing a new way to God through the Christian congregation, no longer fleshly Israel.

We have also learned that God does involve himself miraculously into humankind, but not as often as we are crediting him. When someone claims that a tumor miraculously disappeared, and a child was saved from certain death, we have to recognize rationally that thousands of other children died that same year from brain tumors. In addition, we have to accept rationally that some of the other "miraculous" tumor cases took place with atheists. Moreover, we have to admit that we have only a very minuscule understanding of the mind-body relationship. Finally, we can thank God for the wonderful body and mind that he gave Adam and Eve, which still seems so miraculous in our imperfect condition.

Lastly, we admit that there are times when god does perform miracles on behalf of humankind, but these are exceptional and are for his will and purposes. Let us offer a probable example. William Tyndale published his translation of the English Bible from the original languages of Hebrew and Greek in 1526 (NT), 1530 (OT). The Catholic Church, who sought his death for daring to make a translation, treated him like an outlaw. He accomplished his translation while on the run from the Catholic Church. Like Jesus, a friend with a kiss, Philips, betrayed Tyndale. He finished his translation while being held in captivity. "Tyndale was arrested and imprisoned in the castle of Vilvoorden for over 500 days of horrible conditions. He was tried for heresy and treason in a ridiculously unfair trial, and convicted. Tyndale was then strangled and burnt at the stake in the prison yard, Oct. 6, 1536. His last words were, 'Lord, open the king of England's eyes. This prayer was answered three years later, in the publication of King Henry VIII's 1539 English 'Great Bible.' Tyndale's place in history has not yet been sufficiently recognized as a translator of the Scriptures, as an apostle of liberty, and as a chief promoter of the Reformation in England."[28] Tyndale brought us the first printed English Bible, which was the foundation for the King James Version of 1611. If the reader of this

---

[28] Greatsite.com

http://www.greatsite.com/timeline-english-bible-history/william-tyndale.html

book were to read in detail of the life of William Tyndale, he would see the likelihood of God coming to his aid, to countermove Satan, so that we got the translation that changed the English-speaking world.

If we are to remain rational in our thinking, we need to grasp the fact that God does not always perform miracles when we believe he should or did, nor is he obligated to do so. As was stated earlier, he has greater issues that need resolving, which have eternal effects for the whole of humankind. There are far more times when God does not perform miracles, meaning that our relief may come in the hope of the resurrection. However, for his servants that apply his Word in a balanced manner, fully, God is acting in their best interest by way of his inspired, inerrant Word.

CHAPTER 5 Is Speaking in Tongues Evidence of True Christianity?

An extraordinary gift conveyed through the Holy Spirit to a number of disciples starting at Pentecost 33 C.E. that made it possible for them to speak or otherwise glorify God in a tongue in addition to their own.

What Was the Reason for the Speaking in Tongues?

Immediately before his ascension to heaven, Jesus told those who were looking on: "you will receive power when the Holy Spirit has come upon you, and you will be my witnesses in Jerusalem and in all Judea and Samaria, and to the end of the earth." (Acts 1:8, ESV) First, this witnessing campaign was to be of epic proportions; and second, it was to be brought about with the help of the Holy Spirit.

Our modern-day world allows the spread of the gospel to the other side of the globe within a millisecond and in any language. In the first-century, the good news was spread either in written form, orally, or both. Therefore, the ability to be miraculously able to speak a foreign language in the melting pot of that

Roman Empire would have been greatly appreciated. This miracle was first realized at the Pentecost 33 C.E. celebration, as the first-century Christians began to witness to the Jews and proselytes in Jerusalem.

Acts 2:5-11, 41 English Standard Version (ESV)

5 Now there were dwelling in Jerusalem Jews, devout men from every nation under heaven. 6 And at this sound the multitude came together, and they were bewildered, because each one was hearing them speak in his own language. 7 And they were amazed and astonished, saying, "Are not all these who are speaking Galileans? 8 And how is it that we hear, each of us in his own native language? 9 Parthians and Medes and Elamites and residents of Mesopotamia, Judea and Cappadocia, Pontus and Asia, 10 Phrygia and Pamphylia, Egypt and the parts of Libya belonging to Cyrene, and visitors from Rome, 11 both Jews and proselytes, Cretans and Arabians—we hear them telling in our own tongues the mighty works of God." 41 So those who received his word were baptized, and there were added that day about three thousand souls.

A major change was in the offing. The Jews had followed the lead of their religious leaders in the last act of rebellion, resulting in their rejection as his people. The Mosaic Law was being replaced with the law of Christ. This does not mean that no Jew could be received into the newly founded Christian congregation. To the contrary, the next three and half years would be only the Jewish people, who would make up this new way to God. As was the case with Moses, there was to be a sign, miraculous events, which included the speaking in tongues, this as evidence to those, whose heart was receptive to the truth that the Son of God had come, had given his life for them, and ascended back to heaven. Exodus 19:16-19

Speaking in tongues in Acts 2 is evidentiary. The unique speech is demonstrable proof that something supernatural has happened to the 120 disciples of Jesus. Tongues are the sign that these people have received the promise given by Jesus in Acts 1:5, "You will be baptized with the Holy Spirit not many days from now." This sign was clear enough so that all of those present for the Feast of Weeks were able to see that an impossible event was actually happening. The language speech in this chapter has a second, though subordinate, purpose—

the communication of the gospel to people of a foreign tongue. [29]

However, there was much labor to be done. Beginning in 36 C.E., with the conversion of Cornelius, an uncircumcised Gentile, the gospel got underway in its spread to non-Jewish people of every nation. (Acts, chap. 10) In truth, so swiftly did it spread that by about 60 C.E., the apostle Paul could say that the gospel had been "proclaimed in all creation that is under heaven." (Col. 1:23) Consequently, by the time of the last apostles death (John c. 100 C.E.), Jesus' faithful followers had made disciples all the way through the Roman Empire—in Asia, Europe, and Africa!

---

[29] Chad Brand, "Tongues, Gift Of", in Holman Illustrated Bible Dictionary, ed. Charles Draper, Archie England, Steve Bond et al., 1605 (Nashville, TN: Holman Bible Publishers, 2003).

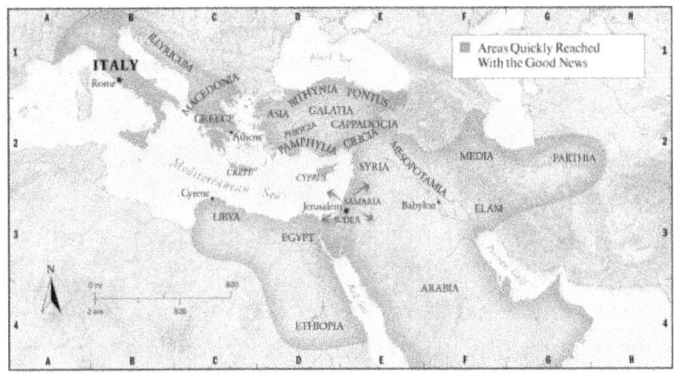

Spread of Christianity in the first century[30]

Modern-day Speaking in Tongues

Among those 'speaking in tongues' today are Pentecostals and Baptists, also Roman Catholics, Episcopalians, Methodists, Lutherans, and Presbyterians. Jesus said, "When the Spirit of truth comes, he will guide you into all the truth …" Would the Pentecostals or the Baptists, who "speak in tongues" suggest that the Roman Catholics, who "speak in tongues" have been 'guided into all the truth,' by the Holy Spirit, as well as the other way around. If modern-day "speaking in tongues" is truly, the

---

[30] (Ac 1:8; 2:1-4, 11; 2:37-41; Ac 5:27, 28, 40-42; 6:7; 8:1, 4, 14-17; 10:1-48; 11:20, 21)

same as the first century, and it is evidence proof that a person has Holy Spirit; then, all of the above groups would equally have to be the true path to God.

There is certainly mixed feeling over the revival of speaking in tongues at the beginning of the 20th century. Many see it as nothing more than excessiveness of unhinged persons, doing nothing more than drawing attention to themselves. On the other hand, many see it as the second Pentecost, identical to the occurrence of speaking with tongues in 33 C.E. There is a difference though for the modern-day counterpart where speaking in unknown tongues occurs. A rapturous explosion of jumbled sounds usually initiates it. Many who have been present at such occasions are unable to understand the chaotic speech, as is the case with all others who are present as well as the speaker himself.

Certainly, any reasonable person is moved to ask 'where the benefit in such unknown tongues is, and where the interpreters are?' It is true that there are some, who claim to interpret this incomprehensible speech, yet here again there exist credibility, because different explanations are offered for the same speech. In an attempt at removing this difficulty, they offer that God has simply given a different interpretation to these ones. However, they are unable to remove the stain that some of this speech has been base, degrading and depraved. Ronald E. Baxter, in his book *Charismatic Gift of Tongues*, mentions an example where a man refused to interpret the speech of a woman who spoke in the so-called 'gift of tongues,' saying, "The language was the vilest of the vile." This is hardly in harmony with the first-century Christian congregation, where tongues were used for "building up the church." 1 Corinthians 14:4-6, 12, 18.

Still, some have heard the interpretation of what they perceive to be a breathtaking message, and believe with their whole heart that God is using this unintelligible speech to give messages to his people. The only problem with this is that Muhammad, Joseph Smith and others make the same kind of argument. The book of Mormon is the supposed second testament of Christ for millions of Mormons. However, like the modern-day speaking in tongues, we are told very clearly to not go beyond what is written, do not add, nor take away, and that there would be no more miraculous messages until after Armageddon, where more books would be made available. Further still, what could be added by the unintelligible speech that is not available by means of Jesus Christ and the apostles through the Greek New Testament: "All Scripture is breathed out by God and profitable for teaching, for reproof, for correction, and for training in righteousness, that the man of God may be competent, equipped for every good work." 2 Timothy 3:16, 17; Deut. 4:12; Gal 1:8; Rev 20:12; 21:18, 19

As is quite clear from the New Testament itself, the gift of tongues was for a congregation that was in its infancy, and was needed for the preaching of the gospel and the building up the church. However, this is no longer the case: "But even if we or an angel from heaven should preach to you a gospel contrary ["at variance with," *The New English Bible*] to the one we preached to you, let him be accursed."—Galatians 1:8.

Thus then, the gift of tongues is no longer needed, and there is no Biblical foundation for supposing that it is an element of modern-day Christianity. In fact, it is unlikely that it ever survived to the middle of the second-century C.E. At present, the Bible is whole and extensively obtainable, and the Word of God is all that we require. This book alone is a road map to an approved relationship with the Father and the Son, which leads to life eternal. John 17:3; Revelation 22:18, 19

The primary verse to consider reads, "For one who speaks in a tongue speaks not to men but to God; for no one understands him, but he utters mysteries in the Spirit." (1 Cor. 14:2, ESV) When considering this verse, he should keep verses 13-19 of the same chapter in mind.

In other words, those who speak in a tongue speak to God as opposed to men **if** he does not have an interpreter for his speech that is to men who are listening. That is to say, the speaking in tongues is meaningless to the men listening, who do not know (understand) the foreign language as given miraculously through the Holy Spirit. It is for this very reason that Paul says, "no one understands." It could also have been that even the speaker himself of the foreign language did not understand what he was saying, because he was not also given the power to interpret (translate). Therefore, without an interpreter, be it himself or another, his speech would only be understood by God, i.e., would be speech only to God, as opposed to men. This is why the apostle Paul would say that if there were no interpreters present, the one speaking in a foreign tongue, should also pray for the gift of interpretation as well. This is so he can speak also to men in a beneficial manner, as well as bring praise to God.

It is Paul, in the first-century, who through the Corinthian congregation sat straight those who had become spellbound and awestruck with the gift of tongues, behaving juvenile, young in the Spirit. While the gift of tongues had its purpose, these ones acted as though it was the most important aspect of the Christian church. (1 Corinthians 14:1-39) The apostle Paul made several things very clear: it was not even a gift that all possessed. Moreover, it did not contribute as an identifying mark of a true Christian, or lead to salvation. Moreover, it was second to the gift of prophecy [proclaiming]. (Elwell, 2001, 1207) Therefore, this gift was not some marker that identified a person as a true Christian, nor was it required to receive the gift of life. 1 Corinthians 12:29, 30; 14:4, 5

What is the Real Force Behind Today's Speaking in Tongues?

There is no doubt that the charismatic church leaders of the 20th century are the impetus behind the resurgence of the speaking in tongues phenomena, pushing their flock members through emotionalism and coercion to achieve this alleged gift. This emotionalist duress is brought on by these church leaders, who exclude any who are unable to speak in tongues, and treat the other members of the church as superior for their ability to speak in tongues. Therefore, the motivating factor is not the Spirit, not to build up the church, not the glorification of God, but to belong.

Should Christians be identified by their ability to "speak in tongues"?

John 13:35 English Standard Version (ESV)

³⁵ By this all people will know that you are my disciples, if you have love for one another."

1 Corinthians 13:1 English Standard Version (ESV)

¹ If I speak in the tongues of men and of angels, but have not love, I am a noisy gong or a clanging cymbal.

Jesus made the Great Commission all too clear when he said, you will receive power when the Holy Spirit has come upon you, and you will be my witnesses in Jerusalem and in all Judea and Samaria, and to the end of the earth." (Ac 1:8) He had instructed them and us to "Go therefore and make disciples of all nations, teaching them" (Matt 28:19-20). Moreover, he had earlier stressed that this was the last sign before the end of this age, by saying, "this gospel of the kingdom will be proclaimed throughout the whole world as a testimony to all nations, and then the end will come." (Matt 24:14) Do we see this being done by the charismatic groups, who advocate "speaking in tongues"? When was the last time you saw a Pentecostal come to your door, proclaiming the Good News? When was the last time you were out, and a Pentecostal witnessed to you? What Pentecostal church have you ever been to that has an evangelism program, to train its members to evangelize their community?

This gift of tongues is possible by mass hysteria. Worse still, the spirit directing this movement may very well not be the Holy Spirit. "She followed Paul and us, crying out, these men are servants of the Most High God, who proclaim to you the way of salvation.' And this she kept doing for many days. Paul, having become greatly annoyed, turned and said to the spirit, 'I command you in the name of Jesus Christ to come out of her.' And it came out that very hour." (Acts 16:17, 18) The apostle Paul cautioned, "Satan disguises himself as an angel of light." (2 Corinthians 11:14) By seeking a Biblical gift that is no more, these ones have made themselves possible victims of "the lawless one [who] is by the activity of Satan with all power and false signs and wonders, and with all wicked deception for those who are perishing, because they refused to love the truth and so be saved." (2 Thessalonians 2:9, 10) However, some might ask:

Does not Mark 16:17, 18 (NKJ) show that the gift of 'speaking with new tongues' would be a sign, so as to recognize believers?

Mark 16:17-18 New King James Version (NKJV)

[17] And these signs will follow those who believe: In My name they will cast out demons; **they will speak with new tongues**; [18] they will take up serpents; and if they drink anything deadly, it will by no means hurt them; they will lay hands on the sick, and they will recover."

First, there is the telling fact that two of the oldest and most highly respected Bible manuscripts, the Vaticanus 03 and the Sinaiticus 01, do not contain this section; they conclude Mark's Gospel with verse eight. This is true of the early versions as well: Syriac, Coptic, Armenian, and Georgian. The early church fathers, Clement, Origen, Cyprian, and Cyril of Jerusalem had no knowledge of anything beyond verse eight. There is little wonder that the noted manuscript authority Dr. Westcott states, "the verses which follow [9-20] are no part of the original narrative but an appendage." Among other noted scholars of the same opinion are Tregelles, Tischendorf, Griesbach, Metzger, and Comfort, to mention just a few.

Adding weight to this evidence of the Greek manuscripts, versions and church fathers are the church historian Eusebius and the Bible translator Jerome. Eusebius wrote that the longer ending was not in the "accurate copies," for "at this point [verse 8] the end of the Gospel according to Mark is determined in nearly all the copies of the Gospel according to Mark." In addition, Jerome, writing about 407 C.E. said, "nearly all Greek MSS have not got this passage."

The vocabulary and style of Mark 16:9-20 vary so drastically from the Gospel of Mark that it scarcely seems possible that Mark himself wrote those verses. Mark's style is plain, direct; his paragraphs are short and the transitions are simple. However, in this ending, there is well-arranged succession of statements, each of them having proper introductory expressions.

Then there is the consideration of the vocabulary of Mark. Verses 9 through 20 contain words that do not appear elsewhere in

Mark's Gospel, and some that do not appear in any of the Gospels, and some still that do not appear in the whole of the Greek New Testament. Verses 9 through 20 contain 163 Greek words, of which, 19 words, 2 phrases do not occur elsewhere in the Gospel of Mark. Looking at it another way, in these 12 verses there are 109 different words, and, of these, 11 words and 2 phrases are exclusive to these 12 verses. Moreover, the doctrinal thesis of Joseph Hug showed that when compared with the vocabulary of the other Gospels, the Apostolic Fathers, and the apocryphal literature, you have 12 verses in "an advanced state of tradition." The note at the end of Metzger's The Text of the New Testament, where I found a summary of Hug's thesis, states:

> The vocabulary suggests that the composition of the ending is appropriately located at the end of the first century or in the middle of the second century. Those who were responsible for adding the verses were intent, not only to supply a suitable ending for the Second Gospel, but also to provide missionary instruction to a Christian Hellenistic community that participated in charismatic activities... (Metzger 1964, 1968, 1992, 297)

The content of these verses also remove them from being considered as original. There is nothing within the whole of the New Testament, which would support the contention in verse 18 that the disciples of Christ were able to drink poison, having no harm come to them. In addition, within this spurious text, you have eleven apostles refusing to believe the testimony of two disciples whom Jesus had come across on the way and to whom he made himself known. However, when the two disciples found the eleven, their reaction was quite different, stating, "The Lord has risen indeed, and has appeared to Simon!" Luke 24:13-35

In summary, Mark 16:9-20 **(1)** is not found in two of the oldest and most highly regarded Greek manuscripts as well as others. **(2)** They are also not found in many of the oldest versions. **(3)** The early church fathers had no knowledge of anything beyond verse eight. **(4)** Such ancient scholars as Eusebius and Jerome marked them spurious. **(5)** The style of these verses is utterly different from that of Mark. **(6)** The vocabulary used in these verses is different from that of Mark. **(7)** Verse 8 does not transition well with verse 9, jumping from the women disciples to Jesus' resurrection appearance. Jesus does not need to appear because Mark ended with the announcement that he had. We only want that because the other Gospels give us an appearance. So we expect it. **(8)** The very content of these verses contradicts the facts and the rest of the Greek New Testament. With textual scholarship, being very well aware of Mark's abrupt style of writing, and abrupt ending to his Gospel does not seem out of place. Eusebius and Jerome, as well as this writer, agree.

Mark 16:17-18 New King James Version (NKJV)

[17] And these signs will follow those who believe: In My name **(1)** they will cast out demons; **(2)** they will speak with new tongues;

(3) ¹⁸ they will take up serpents; and if they drink anything deadly, it will by no means hurt them; **(4)** they will lay hands on the sick, and they will recover."

Is this really, what the Bible teaches?

While Paul was bitten by a poisonous snake and survived, we never find anyone in the New Testament going out to find poisonous snakes, for the purpose of handling them in a religious service. To the contrary, Paul quickly shook off the poisonous snake that had attached itself to his hand. One must ask, 'what purpose would religious snake handling have?' All of the gifts that were bestowed on the first century Christians had a practical purpose. The number one purpose was to evidence to the Jews that the Israelite nation was no longer the way to God, faith in Jesus Christ was.

As for Tongues, They Will Cease

Some may argue that the evidence does not give one any idea of when the gift of tongues was to end. However, they would be mistaken in this case. There are three lines of evidence that present the fact that the gift of tongues would die out shortly after the death of the last apostle, which was the apostle John, who died about 98-100 C.E. **First**, the gift of tongues was always passed on to the person, only by an apostle: either by laying his hands on this one, or at least being present. (Acts 2:4, 14, 17; 10:44-46; 19:6; see also Acts 8:14-18.) **Second**, 1 Corinthians 13:8 informed the Corinthian reader specifically that this gift would "cease." In short, the Greek word for cease [*pausontai*], means to 'peter out,' or 'to die out,' not to be brought to a halt. We will deal with *pausontai* more extensively in a moment. **Third**, both one and two are exactly what happened when we look at the history of this gift of tongues. M'Clintock and Strong's *Cyclopaedia* (Vol. VI, p. 320) says that it is "an uncontested statement that during the first hundred years after the death of the apostles we hear little or nothing of the working of miracles by the early Christians." Therefore, following their passing off the scene and after those who in that way had obtained the gift of tongues breathed their last breath; the gift of tongues should have died out with these ones. (Elwell, 2001, 1207-8) This analysis concurs with the intention of those gifts as acknowledged at Hebrews 2:2-4.

Daniel B. Wallace in his *Greek Grammar Beyond the Basics* helps us to better comprehend how we are to understand *pausontai* of 1 Corinthians 13:8:

If the voice of the verb here is significant, then Paul is saying either that tongues will cut themselves off (direct middle) or, more likely, cease of their own accord, i.e., 'die out' without an intervening agent (indirect middle). It may be significant with reference to prophecy and knowledge, Paul used a different verb ([katargeo]) and out it in the passive voice. In vv 9-10, the argument continues: 'for we *know* in part and we *prophecy* in part; but when the perfect comes, the partial shall be done away with [katargethesontai].' Here again, Paul uses the same passive verb he had used with prophecy and knowledge and he speaks of the verbal counterpart to the nominal 'prophecy' and 'knowledge.' Yet he does not speak about *tongues* being done away 'when the perfect comes.' The implication *may* be that tongues were to have 'died out' on their own *before* the perfect comes. (Wallace 1996, 422)

Speaking in Tongues and Today's Christianity

The gift of tongues "in the NT has three functions: to show the progress of the gift of the Spirit to the various people groups in the book of Acts in a salvation-history context, as a way of revealing the content of the NT revelation, and as a means of communicating cross-linguistically."[31] The apostle Paul made it abundantly clear that the interpretation must be clear and understood for the benefit of all, not the glorification of one. (1 Corinthians 14:26-33) Paul gave a warning: "So with yourselves, if with your tongue you utter speech that is not intelligible, how will anyone know what is said? For you will be speaking into the air." 1 Corinthians 14:9

It is true that many of the early Christians received this gift of tongues by way of Holy Spirit, which did *not* bring forth speech that was incomprehensible or untranslatable nonsense. In accord with Paul's advice, the Holy Spirit made available speech that brought about an

---

[31] Chad Brand, "Tongues, Gift Of", in Holman Illustrated Bible Dictionary, ed. Charles Draper, Archie England, Steve Bond et al., 1606 (Nashville, TN: Holman Bible Publishers, 2003).

outcome in the gospel being "preached in all creation under heaven."—Colossians 1:23.

The church has been attempting with great vigor, to fulfill, Jesus Christ's command of "the gospel must first be proclaimed to all nations." (Mark 13:10) The same as was the case in the first-century, all nations are required to take notice of the message of the ransom death, resurrection and ascension of Christ. This is achievable for the reason that God's Word has now been translated into over 2,300 languages. The unchanged Spirit that instilled the first Christians to speak in tongues is now sustaining the immense and extraordinary commission of the present-day church. 2 Timothy 1:13

Final Thoughts

Certainly, no writer wishes to be arrogantly dogmatic about a belief, an understanding of Scripture that could be overturned or adjusted before his eyes, as he grows in knowledge and understanding. The evidence seems to say that the gift of tongues was given to some in the infant Christian congregation to establish it as the new way to God, to give witness to the mighty acts of God that include the ransom sacrifice of Christ, his resurrection and ascension, and to communicate rapidly to those who spoke other languages.

These abilities were only established by the presence or lying on of hands by the apostles. This coincides with 1 Corinthians 13:8 and the history of these phenomena. Our Greek word for "cease" means that the gift of tongues was to 'die out' over time as the last of those who had received this gift passed off the scene of this earth. This is established by the historical fact that the second century saw just that being evidenced. Today, the Christian is moved by Spirit to speak with his heart and mind, defending and establishing the gospel, and destroying false doctrines, snatching some back from the fire. It is these things, which will give credence to the words of the modern-day Christian congregation: "God is really among you." 1 Corinthians 14:24, 25

CHAPTYER 6 Is Snake Handling Biblical?

Snake handling or serpent handling[32] is a religious ritual in a small number of Pentecostal churches in the U.S., usually characterized as rural and part of the Holiness movement. The practice began in the early 20th century in Appalachia, and plays only a small part in the church service. Practitioners believe serpent-handling dates to antiquity and quote the Gospel of Mark and the Gospel of Luke to support the practice:

Mark 16:17-18 New King James Version (NKJV)[33]

¹⁷ And these signs will follow those who believe: In My name they will cast out demons; they will speak with new tongues; ¹⁸ **they will take up serpents**; and if they drink anything deadly, it will by no means hurt them; they will lay hands on the sick, and they will recover."

---

[32] http://en.wikipedia.org/wiki/Snake_handling

[33] We are using the King James Version throughout this chapter, because that is the only translation the charismatic snake-handlers will use. Therefore, we want you, the reader, to know what their preferred translation says.

Luke 10:19 King James Version (KJV)

¹⁹ Behold, I give unto you **power to tread on serpents** and scorpions, and over all the power of the enemy: and nothing shall by any means hurt you.

Another passage from the New Testament used to support snake handlers' belief is Acts 28:1-6, which relates that Paul was bitten by a venomous viper and suffered no harm. (More on this below)

Founders of Snake Handling

George Went Hensley preaching in 1947 outside a Hamilton County, Tennessee courthouse in which a snake-handling minister was on trial (from Taking Up Serpents: Snake Handlers of Eastern Kentucky by David L. Kimbrough)

George Went Hensley (1880–1955) introduced snake-handling practices into the Church of God Holiness, about 1910.[34] He later resigned his ministry and started the first holiness movement church to require snake

---

[34] Encyclopedia of American Religions gives the year as 1909; the Encyclopedia of Religion in the South gives it as 1913.

handling as evidence of salvation.[35] Sister-churches later sprang up throughout the Appalachian region.[36]

Snake Handlers Today and Practices

As in the early days, worshipers are still encouraged to lay hands on the sick, speak in tongues,[37] provide testimony of miracles, and occasionally consume poisons such as strychnine.[38] Gathering mainly in homes and converted buildings, snake handlers generally adhere to strict dress codes such as uncut hair,

---

[35] Anderson, Robert Mapes (1979). *Vision of the Disinherited: The Making of American Pentecostalism*. New York, New York; Oxford: Oxford University Press. p. 263.

Hood, Jr., Ralph W.; Williamson, W. Paul (2008). *Them That Believe: The Power and the Meaning of the Christian Serpent-Handling Tradition*. Berkeley and Los Angeles, California: University of California Press. pp. xiv, 37, 38.

[36] David L. Kimbrough (February 2002). [Taking up serpents: snake handlers of eastern Kentucky](). Mercer University Press. pp. xiv, 37-51.

[37] See Volume one of *Basic Teachings of the Bible*, Is Speaking in Tongues Evidence of True Christianity?

[38] Dennis Covington, *Salvation on Sand Mountain: Snake Handling and Redemption in Southern Appalachia* (Reading, MA.: Addison-Wesley, 1995).

ankle-length dresses, and no cosmetics for women; and short hair and long-sleeved shirts for men. Most snake handlers preach against any use of tobacco or alcohol.

Most religious snake handlers are still found in the Appalachian Mountains and other parts of the southeastern United States, especially in Alabama, Georgia, Kentucky, North Carolina, Tennessee, West Virginia, and Ohio. However, they are gaining greater recognition due to news broadcasts, movies, and books about the non-denominational movement.

In 2001, about 40 small churches practiced snake handling, most of them considered holiness-Pentecostals or charismatics. In 2004, there were four snake-handling congregations in the provinces of Alberta and British Columbia, Canada. Like their predecessors, today's snake handlers believe in a strict and literal interpretation of the Bible, and most Church of God with Signs Following churches are non-denominational, believing that denominations are human-made and carry the Mark of the Beast. Worshipers attend services several nights a week, where if the Holy Spirit "intervenes," services can last up to five hours, the minimum is usually ninety minutes.

Risks of Snake Handling

Some of the leaders in these churches have been bitten numerous times, as indicated by their distorted extremities. Hensley himself, the founder of modern snake handling in the Appalachian Mountains, died of snakebite in 1955.[39] In 1998, snake-handling evangelist John Wayne "Punkin" Brown died after being bitten by a timber rattlesnake at the Rock House Holiness Church in rural northeastern Alabama[40] although members of his family contend that his death was probably due to a heart attack. Brown's wife had died three years earlier after being bitten in Kentucky. Another snake handler died in 2006 at a church in Kentucky.[41] In 2012, Pentecostal Pastor Mack Wolford died of a rattlesnake bite sustained while officiating

---

[39] Brown, Joi. "Snake Handling in the Pentecostal Church: The Precedent Set by George Hensley". Virginia Tech. Archived from the original on 2005-07-18. Retrieved 2014-01-13.

[40] Custody of 'snake-bite orphans' split between grandparents". CNN. 1999-02-12. Retrieved 2014-01-13.

[41] "Woman fatally bitten by snake in church". USA Today. Associated Press. 2006-11-08. Retrieved 2014-01-13.

at an outdoor service in West Virginia, as did his father in 1983.[42]

Herpetologists have opined that the risk of fatal bites is significantly reduced by the familiarity of the snakes with humans, and by the poor health of snakes that are insufficiently fed and watered.[43]

Does not Mark 16:17, 18 (NKJ) show that 'snake handling' would be a sign that one is a believer?

Mark 16:17-18 New King James Version (NKJV)

17 And these signs will follow those who believe: In My name they will cast out demons; they will speak with new tongues; **18 they will take up serpents**; and if they drink anything deadly, it will by no means hurt them; they will lay hands on the sick, and they will recover."

First, there is the telling fact that two of the oldest and most highly respected Bible

---

[42] Duin, Julia (2012-05-30). "Serpent-handling pastor profiled earlier in Washington Post dies from rattlesnake bite". Washington Post. Retrieved 2014-01-13.

[43] John Burnett (2013-10-18). "Serpent Experts Try To Demystify Pentecostal Snake Handling". National Public Radio.

manuscripts, the Vaticanus 03 and the Sinaiticus 01, do not contain this section; they conclude Mark's Gospel with verse eight. This is true of the early versions as well: Syriac, Coptic, Armenian, and Georgian. The early church fathers, Clement, Origen, Cyprian, and Cyril of Jerusalem had no knowledge of anything beyond verse eight. There is little wonder that the noted manuscript authority Dr. Westcott states, "the verses which follow [9-20] are no part of the original narrative but an appendage." Among other noted scholars of the same opinion are Tregelles, Tischendorf, Griesbach, Metzger, and Comfort, to mention just a few.

Adding weight to this evidence of the Greek manuscripts, versions and church fathers are the church historian Eusebius and the Bible translator Jerome. Eusebius wrote that the longer ending was not in the "accurate copies," for "at this point [verse 8] the end of the Gospel according to Mark is determined in nearly all the copies of the Gospel according to Mark." In addition, Jerome, writing about 407 C.E. said, "nearly all Greek MSS have not got this passage."

The vocabulary and style of Mark 16:9-20 vary so drastically from the Gospel of Mark that it scarcely seems possible that Mark himself wrote those verses. Mark's style is plain, direct; his paragraphs are short and the transitions are simple. However, in this ending, there is well-arranged succession of statements, each of them having proper introductory expressions.

Then there is the consideration of the vocabulary of Mark. Verses 9 through 20 contain words that do not appear elsewhere in Mark's Gospel, and some that do not appear in any of the Gospels, and some still that do not appear in the whole of the Greek New Testament. Verses 9 through 20 contain 163 Greek words, of which, 19 words, 2 phrases do not occur elsewhere in the Gospel of Mark. Looking at it another way, in these 12 verses there are 109 different words, and, of these, 11 words and 2 phrases are exclusive to these 12 verses. Moreover, the doctrinal thesis of Joseph Hug showed that when compared with the vocabulary of the other Gospels, the Apostolic Fathers, and the apocryphal literature, you have 12 verses in "an advanced state of tradition." The note at the end of Metzger's The Text of the New Testament, where I found a summary of Hug's thesis, states:

> The vocabulary suggests that the composition of the ending is appropriately located at the end of the first century or in the middle of the

second century. Those who were responsible for adding the verses were intent, not only to supply a suitable ending for the Second Gospel, but also to provide missionary instruction to a Christian Hellenistic community that participated in charismatic activities... (Metzger 1964, 1968, 1992, 297)

The content of these verses also remove them from being considered as original. There is nothing within the whole of the New Testament, which would support the contention in verse 18 that the disciples of Christ were able to drink poison, having no harm come to them. In addition, within this spurious text, you have eleven apostles refusing to believe the testimony of two disciples whom Jesus had come across on the way and to whom he made himself known. However, when the two disciples found the eleven, their reaction was quite different, stating, "The Lord has risen indeed, and has appeared to Simon!" Luke 24:13-35

In summary, Mark 16:9-20 **(1)** is not found in two of the oldest and most highly regarded Greek manuscripts as well as others. **(2)** They are also not found in many of the oldest versions. **(3)** The early church fathers had no knowledge of anything beyond verse eight. **(4)** Such ancient scholars as Eusebius and Jerome marked them spurious. **(5)** The style of these verses is utterly different from that of Mark. **(6)** The vocabulary used in these verses is different from that of Mark. **(7)** Verse 8 does not transition well with verse 9, jumping from the women disciples to Jesus' resurrection appearance. Jesus does not need to appear because Mark ended with the announcement that he had. We only want that because the other Gospels give us an appearance. So we expect it. **(8)** The very content of these verses contradicts the facts and the rest of the Greek New Testament. With textual scholarship, being very well aware of Mark's abrupt style of writing, and abrupt ending to his Gospel does not seem out of place. Eusebius and Jerome, as well as this writer, agree.

Mark 16:17-18 New King James Version (NKJV)

¹⁷ And these signs will follow those who believe: In My name **(1)** they will cast out demons; **(2)** they will speak with new tongues; **(3)** ¹⁸ they will take up serpents; and if they drink anything deadly, it will by no means hurt them; **(4)** they will lay hands on the sick, and they will recover."

Is This Really, What the Bible Teaches?

While Paul was bitten by a poisonous snake and survived, we never find anyone in the New Testament going out to find poisonous snakes, for the purpose of handling them in a religious service. To the contrary, Paul quickly shook off the poisonous snake that had attached itself to his hand. One must ask, 'what purpose would religious snake handling have?' All of the gifts that were bestowed on the first century Christians had a practical purpose. The number one purpose was to evidence to the Jews that the Israelite nation was no longer the way to God, faith in Jesus Christ was.

"Thou Shall Not Tempt the Lord"

1 John 4:8 in the King James Version reads, "He that loveth not knoweth not God; for God is love." "Symptoms of a venomous snakebite include pain and swelling followed by nausea, vomiting, and weakness. These signs usually emerge within 30 to 60 minutes of the bite, but may also be delayed for several hours."[44] Does it seem like a loving God, who would expect his followers, purposely to inflict pain, suffering and possibly death on themselves?

There is a far greater difference of a God, who expects his followers to be faithful unto death, as opposed to violating Scripture; contrasted with one, who expects his followers

---

[44]

http://www.webmd.com/women/news/20020802/dont-suck-snakebite

needlessly to demonstrate their faith by handling poisonous snakes that can inflict pain and even death. This is especially true, when God can read their heart and mind, and knows whether they are faithful, and would be faithful in a life-threatening situation. Moreover, Christians, who die or suffer pain for their faith, are usually the result of an enemy of God inflicting it on them.

Now, recall the words of Satan to Jesus, "If thou be the Son of God, cast thyself down: for it is written, He shall give his angels charge concerning thee: and in their hands they shall bear thee up, lest at any time thou dash thy foot against a stone." Jesus responded, "It is written again, Thou shalt not tempt the Lord thy God." (Matt 7:6-7) When a minister asks you to test God, or prove your faith, by risking your life in snake-handing, would not Jesus' very words apply? If you test God, are not you demonstrating a lack of faith? Are you not forcing him to carry out your will and purposes of protecting you, upon being bit?

What About Luke 10:19?

Luke 10:19 King James Version (KJV)

¹⁹ Behold, I give unto you **power to tread on serpents** and scorpions, and over all the

power of the enemy: and **nothing shall by any means hurt you**.

If this was meant to be taken literally; then, all of those pastors mentioned above, and far more, would have never suffered in pain, until they died. In addition, no true Christian ever bitten by a poisonous snake or scorpion would have felt the pain of the poison from that bite.

These words have frequently been quoted in close connection with Mark 16:18. A literal interpretation is then given to both passages. At times Acts 28:3 is also cited. But Paul did not deliberately pick up a venomous snake nor did he step on it. As to the authenticity of Mark 16 (16:9–20) see N.T.C. on Mark, pp. 682–687. In the passage now under discussion, namely, Luke 10:19, the figurative explanation is almost certainly the correct one. Note the following:

a. Jesus often made use of figurative language, though such language was frequently interpreted literally (Matt. 16:6–12; Luke 8:52, 53; John 2:19–21; 3:3, 4; 4:13–15;6:51, 52; 11:11–13, etc.).

b. In the immediately preceding passage (verse 18) the Lord had used symbolical language when he spoke of seeing Satan falling from heaven like lightning.

c. If elsewhere Satan is called "dragon" and "serpent" (Rev. 12:9; 20:2), why should it be strange if also here in Luke 10:19 the domain of the prince of evil is called that of snakes and scorpions? Is it not Satan's intention to *poison* the minds of men and to impart the *sting* of death to all who oppose him?

d. There is no record of any *literal* fulfilment of this statement.

e. The true interpretation is also supported by the explanatory expression "(I have given you authority over) ... *all the power of the enemy.*" For explanation see Rom. 16:20, "The God of peace will soon crush Satan under your feet."

As to the promise, "And nothing will in any way hurt you," see John 10:27, 28; Rom. 8:28–39.

In addition, there is no record of snake handling until the modern day charismatic church. If this was meant to be practiced, we would have historical records over an 1800-year period, but we do not. Moreover, the apostle Paul was able to resurrect people from the dead, and he did survive many life-threatening moments, yet he never purposely risked his life, testing or demonstrating his faith, or testing God. (1 Timothy 5:23; 2 Timothy 4:13) Paul did not look for opportunities to resurrect people, to show he had the ability to do so.

What are Christians actually asked to do with their bodies?

Romans 12:1 King James Version (KJV)

¹ I beseech you therefore, brethren, by the mercies of God, that ye present your bodies a living sacrifice, holy, acceptable unto God, which is your reasonable service.

2 Corinthians 13:5 King James Version (KJV)

⁵ Examine yourselves, whether ye be in the faith; prove your own selves. Know ye not your own selves, how that Jesus Christ is in you, except ye be reprobates?

No, we do not risk our lives to 'examine whether we are in the faith,' we rather look at our new Christian personality, making sure that we live by Scripture, evidencing our true Christianity by doing as James said, "faith without works is dead." If we need to test something, it is our doctrinal positions: are they biblical, or just the word of man.

CHAPTER 7 How Are We to Understand the Indwelling of the Holy Spirit?

1 Corinthians 3:16 New American Standard Bible (NASB)

¹⁶ Do you not know that you are a temple of God and *that* the Spirit of God **dwells in you**?

Before delving into the phrase, "indwelling of the Holy Spirit," let us consider the words of New Testament scholars Simon J. Kistemaker and William Hendriksen, who write,

> The Spirit of God lives within you." The church is holy because God's Spirit dwells in the hearts and lives of the believers. In 6:19, Paul indicates that

the Holy Spirit lives in the physical bodies of the believers. But now he tells the Corinthians that the presence of the Spirit is within them and they are the temple of God.

The Corinthians should know that they have received the gift of God's Spirit. Paul had already called attention to the fact that they had not received the spirit of the world but the Spirit of God (2:12). He teaches that Christians are controlled not by sinful human nature but by the Spirit of God, who is dwelling within them (Rom. 8:9).

The behavior—strife, jealousy, immorality, and permissiveness—of the Christians in Corinth was reprehensible. By their conduct the Corinthians were desecrating God's temple and, as Paul writes in another epistle, were grieving the Holy Spirit (Eph. 4:30; compare 1 Thess. 5:19).[45]

First, it must be said that this author is almost amazed at how so many Bible scholars

---

[45] Simon J. Kistemaker and William Hendriksen, *Exposition of the First Epistle to the Corinthians*, vol. 18, New Testament Commentary (Grand Rapids: Baker Book House, 1953–2001), 117

say nonsensical things, contradictory things when it comes to the Holy Spirit. Commentators use many verses to say that the Holy Spirit literally **(1) dwells in** the individual Christian believers, **(2)** having **control over** them, **(3) enabling them** to live a righteous and faithful life,[46] with the believer **(4) still being able to sin**, even to the point of grieving the Holy Spirit (Eph. 4:30).

Let us walk through this again, and please take it slow, ponder whether it makes sense, is reasonable, logical, especially Scriptural. The Holy Spirit literally dwells in individual believers, controlling them so they can live a righteous and faithful life, yet they can still freely sin, even to the point of grieving the Holy Spirit. Does this mean that the Holy Spirit is not powerful enough to prevent their sinful nature from affecting them? The commentators say the Holy Spirit now controls the Christian, not their sinful nature. If that were true, it must mean the Holy Spirit is ineffectual and less powerful than the sinful nature of the Christian, because the Christian can still reject the Holy Spirit and sin to the point of grieving the Holy

---

[46] Millard J. Erickson, *Introducing Christian Doctrine* (Grand Rapids: Baker Book House, 1992), 265–270

Spirit. If the Holy Spirit is controlling the individual Christian, how is it possible that he still possesses free will?

Let us return to the phrase of "indwelling of the Holy Spirit." Just how often do we find "indwelling" in the Bible? Having looked at over fifty English translations, it is found but once in the King James Version and two in the earlier New American Standard Bible. One reference is to sin dwelling within us and the other reference is to the Holy Spirit dwelling within us. The 1995 Updated New American Standard Version removed such usage. We may be asking ourselves, since "indwelling" is almost nonexistent in the Scriptures, why the commentaries, Bible encyclopedias, Hebrew and Greek word dictionaries, Bible dictionaries, pastors, and Christians are using it to such an extent, especially in reference to the Holy Spirit. I say in reference to the Holy Spirit because some scholars refer to the indwelling of Christ and the Word of God.

Before addressing those questions, we must take a look at the Greek word behind 1 Corinthians 3:16 "the Spirit of God **dwells [οἰκέω]** in you." The transliteration of our Greek word is *oikeo*. It means "'to dwell' (from *oikos*, 'a house'), 'to inhabit as one's abode,' is derived from the Sanskrit, *vic*, 'a dwelling place' (the Eng. termination —'wick' is connected). It is used (a) of God as 'dwelling' in light, 1 Tim. 6:16; (b) of the 'indwelling' of the Spirit of God in the believer, Rom. 8:9, 11, or in a church, 1 Cor. 3:16; (c) of the 'indwelling' of sin, Rom. 7:20; (d) of the absence of any good thing in the flesh of the believer, Rom. 7:18; (e) of the 'dwelling' together of those who are married, 1 Cor. 7:12-13."[47]

Thus, for 1 Corinthians 3:16, the Holy Spirit dwelling in true Christians, the TDNT tells us, "Jn.'s μένειν [*menein*] corresponds to Paul's οἰκεῖν [oikein], cf. Jn. 1:33: καταβαῖνον καὶ μένον ἐπ' αὐτόν [descending and remaining upon him]. The new possession of the Spirit is more than ecstatic."[48] What does TDNT mean? It means that John is using meno ("to remain," "to stay" or "to abide") in the same way that Paul is using oikeo ('to dwell').

When we are considering the Father or the Son alone, and even the Father and the Son

---

[47] W. E. Vine, Merrill F. Unger, and William White Jr., *Vine's Complete Expository Dictionary of Old and New Testament Words* (Nashville, TN: T. Nelson, 1996), 180.

[48] Gerhard Kittel, Geoffrey W. Bromiley, and Gerhard Friedrich, eds., *Theological Dictionary of the New Testament* (Grand Rapids, MI: Eerdmans, 1964–).

together, we are able to have a straightforward conversation. However, when we get to the Holy Spirit we tend to get off into mysterious and mystical thinking. When we think of humans and the words *dwell* and *abide*, both have the sense of where we 'live or reside in a place.' However, there is another sense of 'where we might stand on something,' 'our position on something.' Thus, in English "dwell" and "abide" can be used interchangeably, similarly, just as Paul and John use *meno* "abide" or "remain" and *oikeo* "dwell" similarly. Let us look at the apostle John's use of meno,

1 John 4:16 English Standard Version (ESV)

[16] So we have come to know and to believe the love that God has for us. God is love, and whoever **abides [meno]** in love abides in God, and God **abides [meno]** in him.

Here we notice that God is the embodiment of "love" and if we **abide in** or **remain in** that love, God then **abides in** or **remain in** us. We do not attach any mysterious or mystical sense to this verse, such as God literally being in us and us being in God. If we suggest that this verse, i.e., God being in us, means his taking control of our lives, does our being in God, also mean we control his life?

We would think that if one were to suggest such a thing, he is unreasonable, illogical, nonsensical, and such. Commentator Max Anders in the *Holman New Testament Commentary* says, "This is the test of true Christianity in the letters of John. We must recognize the basic character of God, rooted in love. We must experience that love in our own relationship with God. Others must experience this God kind of love in their relationships with us." (Walls and Anders 1999, 211) Our love for God and man is the motivating factor in what we do and not do as Christians. John is saying that we need to remain in that love if we are to remain in God and God is to remain in us. We may be thinking, well, is it not true that God guides and direct us? Yes, however, this is because we have given our lives over to him, and we apply the Spirit inspired, inerrant Word of God in our lives daily.

1 John 2:14 English Standard Version (ESV)

[14] I write to you, fathers,
   because you know him who is from the beginning.
I write to you, young men,
   because you are strong,
   and the word of God abides **[*meno*]** in you,
   and you have overcome the evil one.

Here we see that the Word of God abides or remains in us. Does this mean that the Word of God is literally within our body, controlling us? No, this means that our love for God and our love for his Word is a motivating factor in our walk with God. We are one with the Father as Jesus was and is one with the Father and he is one with us. Listen to the words of Paul in the book of Hebrews,

Hebrews 4:12 English Standard Version (ESV)

¹² For the word of God is living and active, sharper than any two-edged sword, piercing to the division of soul and of spirit, of joints and of marrow, and discerning the thoughts and intentions of the heart.

Is the Word of God literally living, an animate thing? No, it is an inanimate object. Is our Bible literally sharper than a sword? No, if we decide to stab someone with it, it would look quite silly. Is the Word of God literally able to pierce our joints and marrow? No, again, this would look silly. If we literally hold the Bible up to our head, is it able to discern our thinking, what we are intending to do? What did Paul mean? The Word of God does these things by our being able to evaluate ourselves by looking into the light of the

Scriptures, which helps us to identify the intentions of our heart, i.e., the inner person. When we meditatively read God's Word daily and ponder what the author meant, we are taking into our mind, God's thoughts and intentions. When we accept the Bible as the inspired, inerrant Word of God, take its counsel and apply its principles in our lives, it will have an impact on our conscience, the moral code that God gave Adam and Eve, our mental power or ability that enables us to reason as to what is good and what is bad. (Rom 9:1) Then, the inner voice within us is not entirely ours but is also God's Word, empowering us to avoid choosing the wrong path.

1 John 2:24 English Standard Version (ESV)

24 Let what you heard from the beginning **abide [*meno*]** in you. If what you heard from the beginning **abides [*meno*]** in you, then you too will **abide [*meno*]** in the Son and in the Father.

Those who had followed Jesus **from the beginning** of his three and half ministry cleaved to what they had heard about the Father and the Son. Therefore, if the same truths are within our heart, inner person, our mental power or ability, we too can **abide** or **remain [*meno*]** in the Son and the Father. (John 17:3) It is as James said, if we draw close to God, through his Word the Bible, he will draw close to us. (Jam. 4:8) In other words, God becomes a part of us and we a part of him through the Word of God that is "living and active, sharper than any two-edged sword, piercing to the division of soul and of spirit, of joints and of marrow, and discerning the thoughts and intentions of the heart."

In John chapter 14, we see this two-way relationship more closely. Jesus said, "Believe me that I am in the Father and the Father is in me, or else believe on account of the works themselves." **(14:11)** He also said, "In that day you will know that I am in my Father, and you in me, and I in you." **(14:20)** We see that the Father and Son have a close relationship, a relationship that we are invited to join.

All through the above discussion of the Father and the Son, we likely had no problem following the line of thought. However, once we interject the Holy Spirit, it is as though our common sense is thrown out. Christians know that the Father and the Son reside in heaven. They also understand that when we speak of the Word of God, the Father and the Son dwelling in us, it is in reference to our being one with them, our unified relationship, by way of the Word of God. However, when we contemplate the Holy Spirit, it is as though our mental powers shut down, and we enter the realms of the mysterious and mysticism. However, we just understood John **14:11** and **14:20**, i.e., how Jesus is in the Father, the Father in Jesus, and their being in us. So, let us now consider the verses that lie between verse **11** and **20**.

Jesus Promises the Holy Spirit

John 14:15-17 English Standard Version (ESV)

[15] "If you love me, you will keep my commandments. [16] And I will ask the Father,

and he will give you another Helper, to be with you forever, [17] even the Spirit of truth, whom the world cannot receive, because it neither sees him nor knows him. You know him, for he **dwells [meno]** with you and will be in you.

First, do we not find it a bit disconcerting that all along when looking at John's writings as to the Son and the Father abiding **[meno]** in one another, in us, and us in them, the translation rendered **meno** as abiding, but now that the Holy Spirit is mentioned, they render **meno** as "**dwell**."

Do these verses call for us to; drive off the path of reason, into the realms of mysteriousness and mysticism talk? No, these verses are very similar to our 1 John 2:24 that we dealt with above, but will quote again, "Let what you heard from the beginning **abide [meno]** in you. If what you heard from the beginning **abides [meno]** in you, then you too will **abide [meno]** in the Son and in the Father." In 1 John 2:24, we are told that if the Word of God that we heard from the beginning of being a Christian, **abides [meno]** in us, we will **abide [meno]** in the Son and the Father. In John 14:15-17, if we keep Jesus' commands, the Holy Spirit will **dwell**, actually **abide [meno]** in us. In all of this, the common denominator has been the Word of God, because it is what we are to take into our mind and heart, which will affect change in our person, and enable us to abide in the Father and the Son, and they in us, as well as the Holy Spirit abiding in us.

The Holy Spirit, through the Spirit-inspired, inerrant Word of God is the motivating factor for our taking off the old person and putting on the new person. (Eph. 4:20-24; Col. 3:8-9) It is also the tool used by God so that we can 'be transformed by the renewal of our mind, so that we may approve what is the good and well-pleasing and perfect will of God.' (Rom 12:2; See 8:9) *The Theological Dictionary of the New Testament* compares this line of thinking with Paul's reference, at Romans 7:20, to the "sin that dwells within me."

The dwelling of sin in man denotes its dominion over him, its lasting connection with his flesh, and yet also a certain distinction from it. The sin which dwells in me (ἡ οἰκοῦσα ἐν ἐμοὶ ἁμαρτία) is no passing guest, but by its continuous presence becomes the master of the house (cf. Str.-B., III, 239).[49] Paul can speak in just the same way, however, of the lordship of the Spirit. The community knows (οὐκ οἴδατε, a

---

[49] Str.-B. H. L. Strack and P. Billerbeck, *Kommentar zum NT aus Talmud und Midrasch*, 1922 ff.

reference to catechetical instruction, 1 C. 3:16) that the Spirit of God dwells in the new man (ἐν ὑμῖν οἰκεῖ, 1 C. 3:16; R. 8:9, 11). This "dwelling" is more than ecstatic rapture or impulsion by a superior power.[50]

How does the Holy Spirit control a Christian? Certainly, some mysterious or mystical feeling does not control him.

Paul told the Christians in Rome,

Romans 12:2 English Standard Version (ESV)

² Do not be conformed to this world, but be transformed by **the renewal of your mind**, that by testing you may discern what is the will of God, what is good and acceptable and perfect.

---

[50] Gerhard Kittel, Geoffrey W. Bromiley, and Gerhard Friedrich, eds., *Theological Dictionary of the New Testament* (Grand Rapids, MI: Eerdmans, 1964–), 135.

Just how do we **renew our mind**? This is done by taking in an accurate knowledge of Biblical truth, which enables us to meet God's standards of righteousness. (Titus 1:1) This Bible knowledge, if applied, will enable us to move our mind in a different direction, by filling the void, after having removed our former sinful practices, with the principles of God's Word, principles that guide our actions, especially ones that guide moral behavior.

Psalm 119:105 English Standard Version (ESV)

[105] Your word is a lamp to my feet and a light to my path.

The Biblical truths that lay in between Genesis 1:1 and Revelation 22:21 will transform our way of thinking, which will in return affect our mood and actions and our inner person. It will be as the apostle Paul said to the Ephesians. We need to 'to put off our old self, which belongs to our former manner of life and is corrupt through deceitful desires, and to be renewed in the spirit of our minds, and to put on the new self, created after the likeness of God in true righteousness and holiness. . . .' (Ephesians 4:22-24) This force that contributes to our acting or behaving in a certain way, for our best interest is internal.

Paul told the Christians in Colossae,

Colossians 3:9-11 English Standard Version (ESV)

⁹ Do not lie to one another, seeing that you have put off the old self with its practices ¹⁰ and have put on the new self, which is **being renewed in <u>knowledge</u>** after the image of its creator. ¹¹ Here there is not Greek and Jew, circumcised and uncircumcised, barbarian, Scythian, slave, free; but Christ is all, and in all.

Science has certainly taken us a long way in our understanding of how the mind works, but it is only a grain of sand on the beach of sand in comparison to what we do not know. We have enough in these basics to understand some fundamental processes. When we open our eyes to the light of a new morning, it is altered into and electrical charge by the time it arrives at the gray matter of our brain's cerebral cortex. As the sound of the morning birds reaches our gray matter, it arrives as electrical impulses. The rest of our senses (smell, taste, and touch) arrive as electrical currents in the brain's cortex as well. The white matter of our brain lies within the cortex of gray matter, used as a tool to send electrical messages to other cells within other parts of the gray matter. Thus, when anyone of our five senses detects danger, at the speed of light, a message is sent to the motor section, to prepare us for the needed action of either fight or flight.

Here lies the key to altering our way of thinking. Every single thought, whether it is conscious or subconscious makes an electrical path through the white matter of our brain, with a record of the thought and event. This holds true for our actions as well. If it is a repeated way of thinking or acting, it has no need to form a new path; it only digs a deeper, engrained, established path. This would explain how a factory worker who has been on the job for some time, gives little thought as he performs his repetitive functions each day, it becomes unthinking, automatic, mechanical. These repeated actions become habitual. There is yet another facet to be considered; the habits, repeated thoughts, and actions become simple and effortless to repeat. Any new thoughts and actions are harder to perform, as there need to be new pathways opened up.

The human baby starts with a blank slate, with a minimal amount of stable paths built in to survive those first few crucial years. As the boy grows into childhood, there is a flood of pathways established, more than all of the internet connections worldwide. Our five senses are continuously adding to the maze. Ps. 139:14: "I will give thanks to you, for I am fearfully and wonderfully made. . . ." (NASB) So, it could never be overstated as to the importance of the foundational thinking and behavior that should be established in our children from infancy forward.

Paul told the Christians in Ephesus,

Ephesians 4:20-24 English Standard Version (ESV)

[20] But that is not the way you learned Christ!— [21] assuming that you have heard about him and were taught in him, as the truth is in Jesus, [22] to put off your old self, which belongs to your former manner of life and is corrupt through deceitful desires, [23] and to be **renewed in the spirit of your minds**, [24] and to put on the new self, created after the likeness of God in true righteousness and holiness.

How are we to understand being **renewed in the spirit of our minds**? Christian living is carried out through the study and application of God's Word, in which, our spirit (mental disposition), is in harmony with God's Spirit. Our day-to-day decisions are made by a biblical mind, a biblically guided conscience, and a heart that is motivated by love of God and neighbor. Because we have,

- Received the Word of God,
- treasured up the Word of God,
- have been attentive to the Word of God,
- inclining our heart to understanding the Word of God,
- calling out for insight into the Word of God,
- raising our voice for understanding of the Word of God,
- sought the Word of God like silver,
- have searched for the Word of God like gold,
- we have come to understand the fear of God, and have found the very knowledge of God, which now leads and directs us daily in our Christian walk.

Proverbs 23:7 New King James Version (NKJV)

[7] For as he thinks in his heart, so is he. "Eat and drink!" he says to you, But his heart is not with you. [Our thinking affects our emotions, which in turn affects our behavior.]

Irrational thinking produces irrational feelings, which will produce wrong moods, leading to wrong behavior. It may be difficult for each of us to wrap our mind around it, but we are very good at telling ourselves outright lies and half-truths, repeatedly throughout each day. In fact, some of us are so good at it that it has become our reality and leads to mental distress and bad behaviors.

When we couple our leaning toward wrongdoing with the fact that Satan the devil, who is "the god of this world," (2 Co 4:4) has worked to entice these leanings, the desires of the fallen flesh; we are even further removed from our relationship with our loving heavenly Father. During these 'last days, grievous times' has fallen on us as Satan is working all the more to prevent God's once perfect creation to achieve a righteous standing with God and entertaining the hope of eternal life.—2 Timothy 3:1-5.

When we enter the pathway of walking with our God, we will certainly come across resistance from three different areas (Our sinful nature, Satan and demons, and the world that caters to our flesh). Our greatest obstacle is ourselves, because we have inherited imperfection from our first parents Adam and Eve. The Scriptures make it quite clear that we are mentally bent toward bad, not good. (Gen 6:5; 8:21, AT) In other words, our natural desire is toward wrong. Prior to sinning, Adam and Eve were perfect, and they had the natural desire of doing good, and to go against that was to go against the grain of their inner person. Scripture also tells us of our inner person, our heart.

Jeremiah 17:9 Lexham English Bible (LEB)

9 The heart *is* deceitful more than anything else,

and it *is* disastrous. Who can understand it?

Jeremiah's words should serve as a wakeup call, if we are to be pleasing in the eyes of our heavenly Father, we must focus on our inner person. Maybe we have been a Christian for many years; maybe we have a deep knowledge of Scripture, maybe we feel that we are spiritually strong, and nothing will stumble us. Nevertheless, our heart can be enticed by secret desires, where he fails to dismiss them; he eventually commits a serious sin.

Our conscious thinking (aware) and subconscious thinking (present in our mind without our being aware of it) originates in the mind. For good, or for bad, our mind follows certain rules of action, which if entertained one will move even further in that direction until they are eventually consumed for good or for bad. In our imperfect state, our bent thinking will lean toward wrong, especially with Satan using his world, with so many forms of entertainment that simply feeds the flesh.

James 1:14-15 Lexham English Bible (LEB)

14 But each one is tempted *when he*[51] is dragged away and enticed by his own desires. [Or, "caught as by bait." Lit., "being baited on"] **15** Then desire, *after it*[52] has conceived, gives birth to sin, and sin, *when it* is brought to completion, gives birth to death.

1 John 2:16 Lexham English Bible (LEB)

16 because everything *that is* in the world, the desire of the flesh and the desire of the eyes and the arrogance of material possessions—is not from the Father, but is from the world.

Matthew 5:28 Lexham English Bible (LEB)

---

[51] Here "when" is supplied as a component of the participle ("is dragged away") which is understood as temporal

[52] Here "after" is supplied as a component of the participle ("has conceived") which is understood as temporal

28 But I say to you that everyone who looks at a woman to lust for her has already committed adultery with her in his heart.

1 Peter 1:14 Lexham English Bible (LEB)

14 As obedient children, do not be conformed to the former desires *you used to conform to*[53] in your ignorance

If we do not want to be affected by the world of humankind around us, which is alienated from God, we must again consider the words of the Apostle Paul's. He writes (Rom 12:2) "Do not be conformed to this world, but be transformed by the renewal of your mind that by testing you may discern what is the will of God, what is good and acceptable and perfect." Just how do we do that? This is done by taking in an accurate knowledge of Biblical truth, which enables us to meet God's current standards of righteousness. (Titus 1:1) This Bible knowledge, if applied, will enable us to move our mind in a different direction, by filling the void with the principles of God's Word, principles that guide our actions, especially ones that guide moral behavior.

---

[53] This is an understood repetition of the earlier verb "be conformed to"

Psalm 43:3 Updated American Standard Version (UASV)

³ Send out your light and your truth;
 let them lead me;
let them bring me to your holy mountain
 and to your dwelling places!

Bringing This Transformation About

The mind is the mental ability that we use in a conscious way to garner information and to consider ideas and come to conclusions. Therefore, if we perceive our realities based on the information, that surrounds us, generally speaking, most are inundated in a world that reeks of Satan's influence. This means that our perception, our attitude, thoughts, speech and conduct are in opposition to God and his Word. Most are in true ignorance to the changing power of God's Word. The apostle Paul helps us to appreciate the depths of those who reflect this world's disposition. He writes,

Ephesians 4:17-19 Lexham English Bible (LEB)

17 This therefore I say and testify in the Lord, *that* you no longer walk as the Gentiles [unbelievers] walk: in the futility of their mind [emptiness, idleness, vanity, foolishness, purposelessness], **18** being darkened in understanding [mind being the center of human perception], alienated from the life of God [not Godless, but less God], because of the ignorance *that* is in them [due not to a lack of opportunity but deliberate rejection], because of the hardness of their heart [hardening as if by calluses, unfeeling], **19** who, becoming callous, gave themselves over to licentiousness, for the pursuit of all uncleanness in greediness.

Hebrews 4:12 Lexham English Bible (LEB)

¹² For the word of God *is* living and active and sharper than any double-edged sword, and piercing as far as the division of soul and spirit, both joints and marrow, and able to judge the reflections and thoughts of the heart.

By taking in this knowledge of God's Word, we will be altering our way of thinking, which will affect our emotions and behavior, as well as our lives now and for eternity. This Word will influence our minds, making corrections in the way we think. If we are to have the Holy Spirit controlling our lives, we must 'renew our mind' (Rom. 12:2) "which is being renewed in knowledge" (Col. 3:10) of God and his will and purposes. (Matt 7:21-23; See Pro 2:1-6) All of this boils down to each individual Christian digging into the Scriptures in a meditative way, so he can 'discover the knowledge of God, receiving wisdom; from God's mouth, as well as knowledge and understanding.' (Pro. 2:5-6) As he acquires the mind that is inundated with the Word of God, he must also,

James 1:22-25 English Standard Version (ESV)

²² But be doers of the word, and not hearers only, deceiving yourselves. ²³ For if anyone is a hearer of the word and not a doer, he is like a man who looks intently at his natural face in a mirror. ²⁴ For he looks at himself and goes away and at once forgets what he was like. ²⁵ But the one who looks into the perfect law, the law of liberty, and perseveres, being no hearer who forgets but a doer who acts, he will be blessed in his doing.

CHAPTER 8 The Work of the Holy Spirit

BIBLICAL INTERPRETATION IS NOT THE SAME AS SPECULATION

Before we begin unraveling one of the touchiest topics in religious circles, it might be best if we borrow the story from Dr. Robert Stein's book, *A Basic Guide to Interpreting the Bible*:

Tuesday night arrived. Dan and Charlene had invited several of their neighbors to a Bible study, and now they were wondering if anyone would come. Several people had agreed to come, but others had not committed themselves. At 8:00 P.M., beyond all their wildest hopes, everyone who had been invited arrived. After some introductions and neighborhood chit-chat, they all sat down in the living room. Dan explained that he and his wife would like to read through a book of the Bible and discuss the material with the group. He suggested that the book be a Gospel, and, since Mark was the shortest, he recommended it. Everyone agreed, although several said a bit nervously that they really did not know much about the Bible. Dan reassured them that this was all right, for no one present was a "theologian," and they would work together in trying to understand the Bible.

They then went around the room reading Mark 1:1–15 verse by verse. Because of some of the different translations used (the New International Version, the Revised

Standard Version, the King James Version, and the Living Bible), Dan sought to reassure all present that although the wording of the various translations might be different, they all meant the same thing. After they finished reading the passage, each person was to think of a brief summary to describe what the passage meant. After thinking for a few minutes, they began to share their thoughts.

Sally was the first to speak. "What this passage means to me is that everyone needs to be baptized, and I believe that it should be by immersion." John responded, "That's not what I think it means. I think it means that everyone needs to be baptized by the Holy Spirit." Ralph said somewhat timidly, "I am not exactly sure what I should be doing. Should I try to understand what Jesus and John the Baptist meant, or what the passage means to me?" Dan told him that what was important was what the passage meant to him. Encouraged by this, Ralph replied, "Well, what it means to me is that when you really want to meet God you need to go out in the wilderness just as John the Baptist and Jesus did. Life is too busy and hectic. You have to get away and commune with nature. I have a friend who says that to experience God you have to go out in the woods and get in tune with the rocks."

It was Cory who brought the discussion to an abrupt halt. "The Holy Spirit has shown me," he said, "that this passage means that when a person is baptized in the name of Jesus the Holy Spirit will descend upon him like a dove. This is what is called the baptism of the Spirit." Jan replied meekly, "I don't think that's what the meaning is." Cory, however, reassured her that since the Holy Spirit had given him that meaning it must be correct. Jan did not respond to Cory, but it was obvious she did not agree with what he had said. Dan was uncomfortable about the way things were going and sought to resolve the situation. So he said, "Maybe what we are experiencing is an indication of the richness of the Bible. It can mean so many things!"

But does a text of the Bible mean many things? Can a text mean different, even contradictory things? Is there any control over the meaning of biblical texts? Is interpretation controlled by means of individual revelation given by the Holy Spirit? Do the words and grammar control the meaning of the text? If so, what text are we talking about? Is it a particular English translation such as the King James Version or the New International Version? Why not the New Revised Standard Version or the Living Bible? Or why not a German translation such as the Luther Bible? Or should it be the Greek, Hebrew, and Aramaic texts that best reflect what the original authors, such as Isaiah, Paul, and Luke, wrote? And what about the original authors? How are they related to the meaning of the text?

It is obvious that we cannot read the Bible for long before the question arises as to what the Bible "means" and who or what determines that meaning. Neither can we read the Bible without possessing some purpose in reading. In other words, using more technical terminology, everyone who reads the Bible does so with a "hermeneutical" theory in mind. The issue is not whether one has such a theory but whether one's "hermeneutics" is clear or unclear, adequate or inadequate, correct or incorrect. (Stein 1994, p. 12-13)

2 Corinthians 4:3-4 English Standard Version (ESV)

3 And even if our gospel **is veiled**, it is **veiled** to those who are **perishing**. **4** In their case **the god** of this world has **blinded the minds of the unbelievers**,[54] to keep them from seeing the light of the gospel of the glory of Christ, who is the image of God.

---

[54] By **unbelievers** Paul has in view non-Christians (1 Cor. 6:6; 7:12–15; 10:27; 14:22–24). First, the unbelievers of verse 4 are a subset of those who are perishing in verse 3. In other words, the two are the same. Second, the unbelievers are not persons, who have never heard the truth. No, rather, they are persons who have heard the truth, and have rejected it as foolish rubble. This is how this writer is using the term "unbeliever" as well. Technically, how could one ever truly be an unbeliever if they had never heard and understood the truth, to say they did not believe the truth? Therefore, to be an unbeliever, one needs to hear the truth, understand the truth, and reject that truth (i.e., not believing the truth is just that, the truth).

2 Corinthians 3:12-18 English Standard Version (ESV)

¹² Since we have such a hope, we are very bold, **13** not like Moses, who would put a veil over his face so that the Israelites might not gaze at the outcome of what was being brought to an end.¹⁴ But **their minds were <u>hardened</u>**. For to this day, when they read the old covenant, that same **veil remains unlifted**, because only **through Christ is it taken away**. **15** Yes, to this day whenever Moses is read a **veil lies over their <u>hearts</u>**. **16** But **<u>when one turns</u>** to the Lord, the **veil is removed**. 17 Now the Lord is the Spirit, and where the Spirit of the Lord is, there is freedom.**18** And we all, with unveiled face, beholding the glory of the Lord, are being transformed into the same image from one degree of glory to another. For this comes from the Lord who is the Spirit.

Let us start by looking at an example of blind minds within Scripture. This was not a case of physical blindness, but mental blindness. There was a Syrian military force coming after Elisha, and God **blinded them <u>mentally</u>**. If it had been physical blindness, then each of them would have to have been led by hand. However, what does the account say?

2 Kings 6:18-20 American Standard Version (ASV)

¹⁸ And when they came down to him, Elisha prayed to Jehovah, and said, Please strike this people with blindness. And he struck them with blindness according to the word of Elisha. ¹⁹ And Elisha said to them, This is not the way, neither is this the city: follow me, and I will bring you to the man whom you seek. And he led them to Samaria. ²⁰ And it came to pass, when they were come into Samaria, that Elisha said, Jehovah, open the eyes of these men, that they may see. And Jehovah opened their eyes, and they saw; and, behold, they were in the midst of Samaria.

Are we to believe that one man led the entire Syrian military force to Samaria? If they were physically blind, they would have to have all held hands. Were the Syrian military forces not able physically to see the images that were before them? No, rather, it was more of an inability to understand them. This must have been some form of mental blindness, where we see everything that everyone else sees, but something just does not register. Another example can be found in the account about the men of Sodom. When they were blinded, they did not become distressed, running into each other.

Definitely, Paul is speaking of people, who are not receptive to truth, because their heart is hardened to it, callused, unfeeling. They are not responding, because their figurative heart is opposed. It is as though, God handed them over to Satan, to be mentally blinded from the truth, not because he disliked them per se, but because they had closed their hearts and minds to the Gospel. Thus, no manner of argumentation is likely to bring them back to their senses.

HOWEVER, at one time Saul (Paul) was one of these. Until he met the risen Jesus on the road to Damascus, he was mentally blind to the truth. He was well aware of what the coming Messiah was to do, but Jesus did none of these things, because it was not time. Thus, Paul was blinded by his love for the Law, Jewish tradition and history. So much so, he was unable to grasp the Gospel. Not to mention, he lived during the days of Jesus ministry, studied under Gamaliel, who was likely there in the area. He could have even been there when Jesus was amazing the Jewish religious leaders, at the age of twelve. Therefore, Saul (Paul) needed a real wake up call, to get through the veil that blinded him.

Hence, a mentally blind person sees the same information as another, but the truth cannot or will not get down into their heart. I have had the privilege of talking to dozens of small groups of unbelievers, ranging from four people to ten people in my life. I saw this in action. As I spoke to these groups, inevitably, I would see the light going off in the eyes of some (they would be shaking their heads in agreement as I spoke), but others having a cynical look, a doubting look (they would be shaking their heads in disgust or disapproval), and they eventually walked away. This is not saying that the unbeliever cannot understand the Bible; it is simply that they see no significance in it, as it is foolishness to them.

1 Corinthians 2:14 The Lexham English Bible (LEB)

14 But the natural man <u>does not accept</u> the things of the Spirit of God, for <u>they are foolishness</u> to him, and <u>he is **not able to understand**[55] them, because they are spiritually discerned</u>.

Hundreds of millions of Christians use this verse as support that without the "Holy Spirit," we can fully understand God's Word. They would argue that without the "Spirit" the Bible is nothing more than foolish nonsense to the reader. What we need to do before, arriving at the correct meaning of what Paul meant, is grasp what he meant by his use of the word "understand," as to what is 'foolish.' In short, "the things of the Spirit of God" are the "Spirit" inspired Word of God. The natural man sees the inspired Word of God as foolish, and "he is not able to understand them."

---

[55] "The Greek word *ginosko* ("to understand") does not mean comprehend intellectually; it means know by experience. The unsaved obviously do not experience God's Word because they do not welcome it. Only the regenerate have the capacity to welcome and experience the Scriptures, by means of the Holy Spirit."— (Zuck 1991, 23)

Paul wrote, "But the natural man does not accept the things of the Spirit of God, for they are foolishness to him." What did Paul mean by this statement? Did he mean that if the Bible reader did not have the "Spirit" helping him, he would not be able to grasp the correct meaning of the text? Are we to understand Paul as saying that without the "Spirit," the Bible and its teachings are beyond our understanding?

We can gain a measure of understanding as to what Paul meant, by observing how he uses the term "foolishness" elsewhere in the very same letter. At 1 Corinthians 3:19, it is used in the following way, "For the wisdom of this world is foolishness with God." This verse helps us to arrive at the use in two stages: (1) the verse states that human wisdom is foolishness with God, (2) and we know that the use of foolishness here does not mean that God cannot understand (or grasp) human wisdom. The use is that He sees human wisdom as 'foolish' and rejects it as such.

Therefore, the term "foolishness" of 1 Corinthians 3:19 is not in reference to not "understanding," but as to one's view of the text, its significance, or better yet, lack of significance, or lack of value. We certainly know that God can understand the wisdom of the world, but condemns it as being 'foolish.'

The same holds true of 1 Corinthians 1:20, where the verbal form of foolishness is used, "Has not God made foolish the wisdom of the world?" Thus, we have the term "foolishness" being used before and after 1 Corinthians 2:14, (1:20; 3:19). In all three cases, we are dealing with the significance, the value being attributed to something.

Thus, it seems obvious that we should attribute the same meaning to our text in question, 1 Corinthians 2:14. In other words, the Apostle Paul, by his use of the term "foolishness," is not saying that the unbeliever is unable to understand, to grasp the Word of God. If this were the case, why would we ever share the Word of God, the gospel message with an unbeliever? Unbelievers can understand the Word of God; however, unbelievers see it as foolish, having no value or significance. The resultant meaning of chapters 1-3 of 1 Corinthians is that unbelieving world of mankind can understand the Word of God, but views it foolish (lacking value or significance); while God on the other hand understands the wisdom of the world of mankind, but views it foolish (lacking value or significance). Therefore, in both cases, the information is understood or grasped; however, it is rejected because to the party considering it, believes it lacks value or significance.

We pray for the guidance of the Holy Spirit, and our spirit, or mental disposition, needs to be attuned to God and His Spirit through study and application. Now, if our mental disposition is not in tune with the Spirit, we will not come away with the right answer. As Ephesians shows, we can grieve the Spirit.

Ephesians 4:30 English Standard Version (ESV)

³⁰ And do not grieve the Holy Spirit of God, by whom you were sealed for the day of redemption.

How do we grieve the Holy Spirit? We do that by acting contrary to its leading through deception, human weaknesses, imperfections, setting our figurative heart on something other than the leading.

Ephesians 1:18 English Standard Version (ESV)

¹⁸ having the eyes of your hearts enlightened, that you may know what is the hope to which he has called you, what are the riches of his glorious inheritance in the saints,

"Eyes of your heart" is a Hebrew Scripture expression, meaning spiritual insight, to grasp the truth of God's Word. So we could pray for the guidance of God's Spirit, and at the same time, we can explain why there are so many different understandings (many wrong answers), some of which contradict each other, as being human imperfection that is diluting some of those interpreters, causing them to lose the Spirit's guidance.

A person sits down to study and prays earnestly for the guidance of Holy Spirit, that his mental disposition be in harmony with God's Word [or simply that his heart be in harmony with . . .], and sets out to study a chapter, an article, something biblical. In the process of that study, he allows himself to be moved, not by a mental disposition in harmony with the Spirit, but by human imperfection, by way of his wrong worldview, his biases, his preunderstanding.[56] A fundamental of grammatical-historical interpretation is that that we are to look for the simple meaning, the basic meaning, the obvious meaning. However, when this one comes to a text that does not say what he wants it to say, he rationalizes until he has the text in harmony with his

---

[56] Preunderstanding is all of the knowledge and understanding that we possess before we begin the study of the text.

preunderstanding. In other words, he reads his presuppositions into the text, as opposed to discovering the meaning that was in the text. Even though his Christian conscience was tweaked at the true meaning, he ignored it, as well as his mental disposition that could have been in harmony with the Spirit, to get the outcome he wanted.

In another example, it may be that the text does mean what he wants, but this is only because the translation he is using is full of theological bias, which is **violating** grammar and syntax, or maybe textual criticism rules and principles that arrives at the correct reading. Therefore, when this student takes a deeper look, he discovers that it could very well read another way, and likely should because of the context. He buries that evidence beneath his conscience, and never mentions it when this text comes up in a Bible discussion. In other words, he is grieving the Holy Spirit, and loses it on this particular occasion.

Human imperfection, human weakness, theological bias, preunderstanding, and many other things could dilute the Spirit, or even grieve the Spirit, so that while one may be praying for assistance, he is not getting it, or has lost it, because one, some, or all of these things he is doing has grieved the Spirit.

Again, it is not that an unbeliever cannot understand what the Bible means; otherwise, there would be no need to witness to him. Rather, he does not have the spiritual awareness to see the significance of studying Scripture. An unbeliever can look at "the setting in which the Bible books were written and the circumstances involved in the writing," as well as "studying the words and sentences of Scripture in their normal, plain sense," to arrive the meaning of a text. However, without having any spiritual awareness about themselves, they would not see the significance of applying it in their lives. 1 Corinthians 2:14 says, "The natural person does not **accept** [Gr., dechomai] the things of the Spirit of God." Dechomai means, "to welcome, accept or receive." Thus, the unbeliever may very well understand the meaning of a text, but just does not *accept*, *receive* or *welcome* it as truth.

Acts 17:10-11 English Standard Version (ESV)

[10] The brothers immediately sent Paul and Silas away by night to Berea, and when they arrived they went into the Jewish synagogue. [11] Now these Jews [the Beroeans] were more noble than those in Thessalonica; they received [dechomai] the word with all eagerness,

examining the Scriptures daily to see if these things were so.

Unlike the natural person, the Beroeans accepted, received, or welcomed the Word of God eagerly. Paul said the Thessalonians "received [*dechomai*] the word in much affliction, with the joy of the Holy Spirit." (1 Thess. 1:6) In the beginning of a person's introduction to the good news, he will take in knowledge of the Scriptures (1 Tim. 2:3-4), which if his heart is receptive, he will begin to apply them in his life, taking off the old person and putting on the new person. (Eph. 4:22-24) Seeing how the Scriptures have begun to alter his life, he will start to have a genuine faith over the things he has learned (Heb. 11:6), repenting of his sins. (Acts 17:30-31) He will turn around his life, and his sins will be blotted out. (Acts 3:19) At some point, he will go to God in prayer, telling the Father that he is dedicating his life to him, to carry out his will and purposes. (Matt. 16:24; 22:37) This regeneration is the Holy Spirit working in his life, giving him a new nature, placing him on the path to salvation.—2 Corinthians 5:17.

A new believer will become "acquainted with the sacred writings, which are able to make [him] wise for salvation through faith in Christ Jesus." (2 Tim. 3:15) As the Bible informs us, the Scriptures are holy, and are to be viewed as such. If we are to acquire an accurate or full knowledge, to have the correct mental grasp of the things that we carried out an exegetical analysis on, it must be done with a prayerful and humble heart. It is as Dr. Norman L. Geisler said, "the role of the Holy Spirit, at least in His special work on believers related to Scripture, is in illuminating our understanding of the significance (not the meaning) of the text. The meaning is clear apart from any special work of the Holy Spirit." What level of understanding that we are able to acquire is based on the degree to which we are **not** grieving the Holy Spirit with our worldview, our preunderstanding, our presuppositions, our theological biases. In addition, anyone living in sin will struggle to grasp God's Word as well.

No interpreter is infallible. The only infallibility or inerrancy belonged to the original manuscripts. Each Christian has the right to interpret God's Word, to discover what it means, but this does not guarantee that they will come away with the correct meaning. The Holy Spirit will guide us into and through the truth, by way of our working in behalf of our prayers to have the correct understanding. Our working in harmony with the Holy Spirit means that we buy out the time for a personal study program, not to mention the time to prepare properly and carefully for our Christian meetings. In these studies, do not expect that the Holy Spirit is going to miraculously give us some flash of understanding, but rather understanding will come to us as we set aside our personal biases, worldviews, human imperfections, presuppositions, preunderstanding, opening our mental disposition to the Spirit's leading as we study.

The Work of the Holy Spirit

The following is adopted and adapted from Douglas A. Foster of Abilene Christian University.

Christian Publishing House's understanding of the Holy Spirit is **not** that of the Charismatic groups (the ecstatic and irrational), but rather the calm and rational. The work of the Holy Spirit is inseparably and uniquely linked to the words and ideas of God's inspired and inerrant Word. We see the indwelling of the Holy Spirit as Christians taking the words and ideas of Scripture into our mind and drawing spiritual strength from them. The Spirit moves persons toward salvation, but the Spirit does that, in the same way, any person moves another—by persuasion with words and ideas:

> Now we cannot separate the Spirit and the Word of God, and ascribe so much power to the one and so much to the other; for so did not the Apostles. Whatever the word does, the Spirit does, and whatever the Spirit does in the work of converting, the word does. We neither believe nor teach abstract Spirit nor abstract word, but word and Spirit, Spirit and word. But the Spirit is not promised to any persons outside of Christ. It is promised only to them who believe and obey him.[57]

The Holy Spirit works only through the word in the conversion of sinners. In other words, the Spirit acting through the Word of God can accomplish everything claimed to be effected by a personal indwelling of the Spirit.

longtime preacher Z. T. (Zachary Taylor) Sweeney, in His book *The Spirit and the Word: A Treatise on the Holy Spirit in the Light of a Rational Interpretation of the Word of God*,

---

[57] Alexander Campbell, The Christian System (6th ed.; Cincinnati: Standard, 1850), 64.

writes after examining every Scripture that might be used by advocates of a literal personal indwelling of the Holy Spirit,

> In the above cases, we have covered all the conceivable things a direct indwelling Spirit could do for one, and have also shown that all these things the Spirit does through the word of God. It is not claimed that a direct indwelling of the Spirit makes any new revelations, adds any new reasons or offers any new motives than are found in the word of God. Of what use, then, would a direct indwelling Spirit be? God makes nothing in vain. We are necessarily, therefore, led to the conclusion that, in dealing with his children today, God deals with them in the same psychological way that he deals with men in inducing them to become children. This conclusion is strengthened by the utter absence of any test by which we could know the Spirit dwells in us, if such were the case.[58]

---

[58] Z. T. Sweeney, The Spirit and the Word (Nashville: Gospel Advocate, n.d.), 121–26.

Christian Publishing House is defined by our rejection of Holiness and Pentecostal understandings of the Holy Spirit. The Holy Spirit transforms a person, empowering him through the Word of God, to put on the "new person" required of true Christians: "So, as those who have been chosen of God, holy and beloved, put on a heart of compassion, kindness, humility, gentleness and patience."—Col. 3:12.

Ephesians 4:20-24 English Standard Version (ESV)

[20] But that is not the way you learned Christ!—[21] assuming that you have heard about him and were taught in him, as the truth is in Jesus, [22] to put off your old self, which belongs to your former manner of life and is corrupt through deceitful desires, [23] and to be renewed in the spirit of your minds, [24] and to put on the new self, created after the likeness of God in true righteousness and holiness.

Colossians 3:9-10 English Standard Version (ESV)

[9] Do not lie to one another, seeing that you have put off the old self with its practices [10] and have put on the new self, which is being renewed in knowledge after the image of its creator.

Bibliography

Anders, Max, and Steven Lawson. *Holman Old Testament Commentary - Psalms: 11.* Grand Rapids: B&H Publishing, 2004.

Bercot, David W. *A Dictionary of Early Christian Beliefs.* Peabody: Hendrickson, 1998.

Brand, Chad, Charles Draper, and England Archie. *Holman Illustrated Bible Dictionary: Revised, Updated and Expanded.* Nashville, TN: Holman, 2003.

Bromiley, Geoffrey W. *The International Standard Bible Encyclopedia (Vol. 1-4).* Grand Rapids, MI: William B. Eerdmans Publishing Co., 1986.

Campbell, Alexander. *The Christian System (6th ed.;.* Cincinnati: Standard, 1850.

Elwell, Walter A. *Baker Encyclopedia of the Bible.* Grand Rapids: Baker Book House, 1988.

—. *Evangelical Dictionary of Theology (Second Edition).* Grand Rapids: Baker Academic, 2001.

Elwell, Walter A, and Philip Wesley Comfort. *Tyndale Bible Dictionary*. Wheaton, Ill: Tyndale House Publishers, 2001.

Enns, Paul P. *The Moody Handbook of Theology*. Chicago: Moody Press, 1997.

Erickson, Millard J. *Introducing Christian Doctrine*. Grand Rapids: Baker Book Hous, 1992.

Erickson, Milliard J. *Christian Theology*. Grand Rapids, MI: Baker Academic, 1998.

Green, Joel B, Scot McKnight, and Howard Marshall. *Dictionary of Jesus and the Gospels*. Downers Grove, IL: InterVarsity Press, 1992.

Gruden, Wayne. *Are Miraculous Gifts for Today?: 4 Views (Counterpoints: Bible and Theology)*. Grand Rapids: Zondervan, 2011.

Kistemaker, Simon J., and William Hendriksen. *Exposition of the First Epistle to the Corinthians, vol. 18, New Testament Commentary*. Grand Rapids, MI: Baker Book House, 1953–2001.

Kittel, Gerhard, Gerhard Friedrich, and Geoffrey William Bromiley. *Theological Dictionary of the New Testament*. Grand Rapids: Eerdmans, 1995, c1985.

Microsoft. *Encarta ® World English Dictionary.* Redmond: Microsoft Corporation, 1998-2010.

Mirriam-Webster, Inc. *Mirriam-Webster's Collegiate Dictionary. Eleventh Edition.* Springfield: Mirriam-Webster, Inc., 2003.

Mounce, William D. *Mounce's Complete Expository Dictionary of Old & New Testament Words.* Grand Rapids, MI: Zondervan, 2006.

Stein, Robert H. *A Basic Guide to Interpreting the Bible: Playing by the Rules.* Grand Rapids: Baker Books, 1994.

Sweeney, Z. T. *The Spirit and the Word (: , n.d.), 121–26.* Nashville: Gospel Advocate, 2005.

Towns, Elmer L. *Theology for Today.* Belmont: Wadsworth Group, 2002.

Vine, W E. *Vine's Expository Dictionary of Old and New Testament Words.* Nashville: Thomas Nelson, 1996.

Wood, D R W. *New Bible Dictionary (Third Edition).* Downers Grove: InterVarsity Press, 1996.

Zodhiates, Spiros. *The Complete Word Study Dictionary: New Testament.*

Chattanooga: AMG Publishers, 2000, c1992, c1993.

www.ingramcontent.com/pod-product-compliance
Lightning Source LLC
Chambersburg PA
CBHW020000050426
42450CB00005B/265